CLOSE ENCOUNTERS

Books by Warren Agius

Evidence of Extraterrestrials: Over 40 Cases Prove Aliens Have Visited Earth
(Llewellyn Worldwide, 2021).

CLOSE ENCOUNTERS
Exploring the Mysteries
of Alien Abductions

Warren Agius

AEON

First published in 2024 by
Aeon Books

British Library Cataloguing in Publication Data

A C.I.P. for this book is available from the British Library

ISBN-13: 978-1-80152-141-3

Typeset by Medlar Publishing Solutions Pvt Ltd, India

www.aeonbooks.co.uk

*To Laura, my better half and constant source
of inspiration and support.*

Ad Astra

"not only are we not central in the scheme of things, but we may be inferior, physically, mentally and spiritually, to more highly evolved beings elsewhere."[1]

---

[1] Walter Sullivan, *We Are Not Alone: The Search for Intelligent Life on Other Worlds* (New York: McGraw-Hill, 1970).

CONTENTS

PREFACE

In recent years, there has been a significant shift in how the public views Unidentified Anomalous Phenomena (UAP). As a matter of fact, we generally now use the term UAP, not UFOs (with that being said, the two terms will be used interchangeably throughout this book). Although some may not see the significance, the introduction of the term UAP highlights a shift in how the government views the UFO phenomenon. The wave of disclosure and greater transparency began in December 2017 when three very important videos (titled FLIR, GIMBAL, and Go Fast) were leaked by *The New York Times*. These three videos showed military fighter jets pursuing UFOs. Those of us who have a great interest in the phenomenon are well aware that the military has always taken UFOs seriously, but these videos demonstrated to the general public that military pilots have indeed been seeing and pursuing UFOs. It was no longer a conspiracy theory; it became public knowledge.

We have come a long way since the days of Project Sign and Project Blue Book, when the majority of UFO cases were dismissed and given illogical and contradictory explanations. Now, the government has publicly admitted that UFOs exist, that these aircraft are in possession of advanced technology, and even pose a threat to our national security. In addition to this, the aircraft in the three videos reaffirmed the idea that these unidentified aircraft, which the military has been investigating for decades, defy the laws of physics and aerodynamics—laws that every terrestrial aircraft is bound by. Thus, 2017 was a significant year in the study of UFOs and marked the beginning of a journey towards transparency and disclosure.

The phenomenon received more public attention than ever before in the years that followed, as numerous credible military personnel came forward and shared their stories about the close encounters they had experienced with UAP throughout their careers. The correlation between UFOs and these sightings occurring over military airspace became clearer, and one of the most plausible explanations for this occurrence is that these aircraft and beings are especially interested in monitoring our military activity. One of the most notable accounts was that of Commander David Fravor, who in 2004 chased down a tic-tac shaped UFO, the same aircraft seen in the FLIR footage. Commander Fravor's story has revolutionized the UFO phenomenon and is certainly one of the most important UFO cases to date.

In June 2021, the Director of Intelligence issued a report on UAP, and in it, several significant claims were made. First, the report acknowledged that these UFOs are real, physical aircraft and had been recorded on a number of instruments, including radar, infrared, electro-optical, and weapon seeker sensors. This ruled out the possibility that UFOs were either illusions or natural phenomena, as many skeptics had been claiming for so many years. Second, the report stated that UAP maneuver in ways which demonstrate that they have advanced technology—technology which allows them to defy the laws of physics and aerodynamics. The third implication is perhaps the most crucial one: the report stated that on numerous occasions, UAP have infiltrated national and military airspace and even disrupted military activity. This poses a significant threat to national security and it is imperative that it is addressed with the highest of priorities. This is made even more concerning by the report's confirmation that these aircraft were neither Russian nor Chinese. Their true origin is unknown. This fact is alarming, and the Department of Defense has acknowledged the gravity of the situation.

I will present data below indicating that the Air Force and its component organizations actually detected thousands of UAP from 2004 through 2021. Admittedly, it is theoretically conceivable that

none represented breakthrough Russian or Chinese technology—
much less alien spacecraft—but the point is that we simply don't
know. That's what makes them UAP.[2]

Disclosure is continually happening, and for the first time in fifty years,
in May 2022, the United States House Intelligence Subcommittee on
Counterterrorism, Counterintelligence and Counterproliferation held
a congressional hearing on UAP reports made by military personnel.
During the hearing, several military officials discussed their experience
with UFOs throughout their careers. Two officials in particular stated
that they experienced eleven near-collisions with unidentified aircraft.
Eleven! The hearings concluded that the military was now required to
establish a permanent office to investigate UAP reports, the name of the
office being the Airborne Object Identification and Management Syn-
chronization Group. We have come a long way indeed.

Unidentified aerial phenomena are a potential national security
threat. And they need to be treated that way.[3]

This brings me to why I felt the need to write this book. In 2021, my first
book, titled *Evidence of Extraterrestrials: Over 40 Cases Prove Aliens Have
Visited Earth* was published, and in it I explore and analyze the most significant UFO sightings in history. During the course of writing the book,
I learned that it was highly unlikely, if not impossible, for these aircraft
to be of terrestrial origin. Their characteristics, maneuverability, and
capabilities are just astounding. After the book was published, many
individuals from all around the world reached out to me to tell me
about their own UFO sightings and experiences, and that showed me
that the book had reached its objective: it helped to create and continue
a dialogue about the UFO phenomenon. Having these conversations
solidified the fact that this phenomenon occurs on a global scale. Having said that, while the cases covered in the book are enthralling, I knew
there was another phenomenon I wanted to investigate that is equally,

---

[2] Christopher Mellon, "Why Is The Air Force Awol On The Uap Issue?", *The Debrief*,
February 2022. https://thedebrief.org/why-is-the-air-force-awol-on-the-uap-issue/.
[3] Permanent Select Committee on Intelligence: Subcommittee on Counterterrorism,
Counterintelligence, and Counterproliferation, "Unidentified Aerial Phenomena, D545".
Congressional Record—Daily Digest, May 2022. https://govinfo.gov/content/pkg/
CREC-2022-05-17/pdf/CREC-2022-05-17-pt1-PgD545-2.pdf#page=1.

if not more, perplexing and intriguing: close encounters. While in the first book I explored UFO cases which prove that Earth is being visited by extraterrestrials, in this book I will explore the more sinister phenomenon of alien abductions. The cases that follow show that a number of people have had close encounters with these beings, and they have been observing and experimenting on human beings for decades. Why extraterrestrials are so intrigued and interested in us, however, we can only speculate.

As I was carrying out research for this book it became evident that if genuine UFO sightings are rare, alien abduction cases are even more so. I have read of countless cases which were evidently a hoax or a quick attempt for fame and money, and unfortunately, it is these cases which cast a negative light on this phenomenon and lead people to believe that alien abductions only happen in sci-fi movies. As this book will prove, that is not the case—genuine alien abductions occur and there is ample evidence to prove this. Aside from alien abductions, I also wanted to cover close encounters of the third kind, which refer to cases in which although the individual was not abducted, they were in close proximity to an extraterrestrial aircraft and witnessed an extraterrestrial entity. Close encounters of the third and fourth kind (abductions) differ significantly from UAP sightings; aside from the nature of the experience, while it is possible to conclusively determine the authenticity of a UAP sighting (through radar readings for instance), proving whether or not an alien abduction occurred is not as simple. To determine the veracity of a case, several factors must be considered, including the individual's background, other plausible hypotheses, and the supporting evidence for each theory. Throughout the writing of this book I ensured that every detail is presented accurately, and that no aspect is sensationalized in an attempt to prove the extraterrestrial hypothesis. The intention of this book is not to convince you that alien abductions happen, as a matter of fact, in each chapter I will present a number of potential hypotheses. The aim of this book is to make you ponder on this possibility and give you all the information necessary to help you come to an informed opinion on the matter.

Before we delve into these fascinating phenomena, I would like to share one final thought: there is so much more to this topic than just a fascinating narrative. Naturally, close encounters make for a thrilling and compelling narrative, but these phenomena are far more complex than just that. There are spiritual, philosophical, and existential implications which affect us as a human race collectively. I hope that the following cases will be as intriguing and eye-opening for you as they were for me. I hope they will make you question what it means to be human and why our planet and existence is so important for these beings. Finally, I hope this book inspires you to look up at the dark cosmos more often and make you wonder what it means to share this infinite universe with other intelligent and conscious life-forms.

INTRODUCTION

The cases and phenomena discussed in this book are incredibly fascinating and captivating, and as has been demonstrated over time, these extraterrestrial beings are far more advanced than we are. As stated in the Preface of this book, there is far more to close encounters than just a gripping story. The phenomenon has several consequential implications, some of which will be discussed in greater depth in this book. Before moving on to the cases, we will look at two of these implications: The fact that alien abductions occur implies that:

a) Intelligent, conscious, and advanced life-forms exist outside of Earth.
b) Since these life-forms originate outside of Earth, interstellar travel is possible.

Implication #1: The existence of intelligent and conscious extraterrestrial life

> We believe that life arose spontaneously on Earth. So, in an infinite universe, there must be other occurrences of life. Somewhere in the cosmos, perhaps, intelligent life may be watching these lights of ours, aware of what they mean…. there is no bigger question. It is time to commit to find the answer—Stephen Hawking, 2015.[4]

What is the likelihood that an advanced and conscious life-form exists elsewhere in the universe? In 2014 NASA initiated a study named the Ultraviolet Coverage of the Hubble Ultra Deep Field. In this study, with the use of ultraviolet light, astronomers were able to capture an impeccable image of the evolving universe. This image alone depicts nearly 10,000 galaxies, some of which date back to only a few million years after the big bang took place.

> This view of nearly 10,000 galaxies is called the Hubble Ultra Deep Field. The snapshot includes galaxies of various ages, sizes, shapes, and colors. The smallest, reddest galaxies, about 100, may be among the most distant known, existing when the universe was just 800 million years old. The nearest galaxies—the larger, brighter, well-defined spirals and ellipticals—thrived about 1 billion years ago, when the cosmos was 13 billion years old.[5]

In reality, the existence of 10,000 galaxies is already unfathomable and difficult to comprehend, but this is only just a small fraction of what exists. To capture the Hubble Ultra Deep Field, the telescope was aimed at a very small fraction of space; thus, the actual number of galaxies is remarkably higher than that. If you are finding it difficult to wrap your head around this (as am I), Dr. Edward Weiler, the former chief scientist for the Hubble Space Telescope program explained it perfectly with the following analogy:

---

[4] Breakthrough Initiatives. "Launch of Breakthrough Initiatives". *Breakthrough Initiatives*. July 2015. https://breakthroughinitiatives.org/events/4.
[5] European Space Agency. "Hubble Sees Galaxies Galore". *ESA Science and Technology*. November 2022. https://sci.esa.int/s/WEqe0EW.

If you want a human analogy, go out on a clear night, get a standard
sewing needle, hold it up at arms' length and look at the hole in the
sewing needle. That's the size of the sky you're seeing portrayed
here.[6]

As technology advances and humans make greater leaps in space
exploration, we are gaining more precise information about the ever-
expanding universe. Dr. Christopher Conselience, an astrophysics
professor at the University of Nottingham, conducted a research
study in 2016 using Hubble telescope images from deep space. These
images revealed that there are at least two trillion galaxies—ten times
what they had previously estimated. That's right, two trillion galaxies. Keeping this astronomical number in mind, would it not be somewhat preposterous to believe that human life is the only intelligent life
out there?

The Drake equation

There is nothing more factual than data, and Dr. Frank Drake, an astronomer and astrophysicist, began his quest for certainty in 1961, when he,
together with a number of experts in the field, developed a formula that
when its values are added, gives an estimation of how many commu-
nicative, intelligent civilizations exist in our galaxy. This meeting was
also a pivotal moment in the scientific community as it was the first
time a group of scientists sat down together to explore and discuss the
existence of extraterrestrial life. The members included Dr. Drake himself, conference organizer Peter Pearman, physics professor and nuclear
physics and astrophysics expert Philip Morrison, radio astronomer
Dana Atchley, biochemist and Nobel Prize winner Melvin Calvin, astrophysicist Si-Shu Hu, neuroscientist John Lilly, scientist Barney Oliver,
astronomer Otto Stuve, and lastly, renowned astronomer, cosmologist,
and astrophysicist Carl Sagan.

The equation that the members devised is as follows:

$$N = R_* \cdot f_p \cdot n_e \cdot f_l \cdot f_i \cdot f_c \cdot L$$

[6]NASA Goddard Media Studios, "NASM 2015: Our Violent Universe." NASA Goddard
Media Studios. November 2015. https://svs.gsfc.nasa.gov/12027.

Where:

N = Represents the number of potential intelligent extraterrestrial civilizations.

R_* = Represents the average rate of star formation in a year.

f_p = Represents those stars which contain planets.

n_e = Represents those planets which could potentially sustain life.

f_l = Represents the estimated number of planets on which life does actually evolve (implying that these planets have an environment that supports and sustains the evolution of life).

f_i = Represents the fraction number of planets on which intelligent life emerges.

f_c = Represents the fraction number of planets which sustain intelligent life, but also develop a detectable means of communication.

L = Represents the longevity of the detectable communication.

As one might expect, these factors do not contain one singular value. Thus, Drake and the other experts used estimates and calculated a minimum and maximum value.

$R_* = 1$ yr^{-1} Meaning that over the life of a galaxy, one star per year is formed.

$f_p = 0.2$ to 0.5 Meaning that only one fifth to one half of the developed stars will have planets.

$n_e = 1$ to 5 Meaning that out of those stars with planets, only 1 to 5 are able to sustain life.

$f_l = 1$ Meaning that out of these planets, all of them will develop life.

$f_i = 1$ Meaning that out of these planets, all of the developed life will be intelligent.

$f_c = 0.1 - 0.2$ Meaning that out of the developed intelligent life, 10 to 20% of it will be able to communicate.

$L = 1,000$ to $1000,000,000$ civilizations.

Once the members agreed on the formula and the estimated values, they computed the formula twice, using the lowest and highest values. When using the lowest value, the answer was 20, meaning that there are an estimated 20 intelligent extraterrestrial civilizations. When using the higher value, the answer was 50,000,000. Due to the discrepancies, Dr. Drake concluded there to be between 1,000 and 100,000,000 planets in the Milky Way which contain and can sustain the evolution of an intelligent civilization.[7]

The Drake Equation has been the subject of several debates over the years. The formula is undeniably overly simplistic, makes a number of assumptions, and its values are an estimate at best. The importance of the Drake Equation has less to do with the numbers and more to do with the dialogue it created. For the first time in scientific history, experts acknowledged the sheer vastness of the universe and the likelihood that extraterrestrial life exists. These astronomical values made us stop and ponder on this possibility and that we are very likely to be sharing the universe with other intelligent and conscious life-forms. We do not need a formula to prove this, especially nowadays. More data is being released all the time demonstrating that the universe is brimming with life and Earth is just one speck on an infinitely sized canvas.

So, if extraterrestrial life exists and has visited our planet, this implies that interstellar travel is conceivable. This is the second implication which we shall now explore.

▲ ▼ ▲

Implication #2: Interstellar travel

Interstellar travel was once considered to be strictly a sci-fi concept, but we now know that this is not the case and that it can be achieved. To explore this further, we must keep in mind Einstein's theory of general relativity and the fact that as gravity increases, the more space-time bends, causing time to slow down. This means that if we can manipulate gravity, we can also manipulate space and time. As a result, an anti-gravitational propulsion system (i.e. an aircraft that generates its own gravitational field) makes interstellar travel a real possibility. The military has been interested in anti-gravitational technology for decades, and understandably so. Imagine how unstoppable a nation would become if it was in possession of this advanced technology. The Defense Intelligence Agency, as part of the Advanced Aerospace Weapon System Applications (AAWSA), explored anti-gravity technology and how it could be potentially utilized for aerospace propulsion. It is undeniable

---

[7] Dava Sobel and Frank Drake. *Is Anyone Out There? The Scientific Search for Extraterrestrial Intelligence* (New York: Delacorte Press, 1992).

that having such technology would put any country at the forefront of space exploration. The main premises behind anti-gravity technology are the following:

- Anti-gravity refers to any force produced that opposes Earth's gravitational pull.
- If we manipulate gravity, we also manipulate space-time.
- If an aircraft has an anti-gravitational propulsion system that generates its own gravitational field and manipulates space-time, the aircraft is able to travel long distances in exponentially less time.

Theoretically, at the current moment, anti-gravity is purely hypothetical as no government has stated that they are in possession of such technology (even if they were, it is unlikely they would disclose this). However, there are reasons to believe that this is not the case. In May 1989, one man in particular came forward and stated that the military was working on reverse engineering alien technology, which included an anti-gravitational propulsion system. The man is named Bob Lazar, and I will refer to his extraordinary testimony to further explore interstellar travel.

Bob Lazar's story

In May 1989, an individual using the pseudonym Dennis appeared on KLAS and stated that he worked in a secluded site known as "S-4," which is a facility located a few miles off the Nevada Test and Training Range, Area 51. The facility is intelligently built into a mountainside so that satellites are unable to detect its presence. Later on, Dennis's true identity was revealed; it was a man named Robert Lazar. Over the course of a few weeks, Bob was interviewed by renowned reporter George Knapp, during which Bob revealed that the United States government was in possession of a recovered alien aircraft and his job was to reverse engineer the alien technology. The following is Lazar's description of how the aircraft operates.

The aircraft

At S-4, Lazar stated that he worked on a disk-shaped aircraft which he referred to as the "Sport Model." The propulsion system of this aircraft has three main components: the reactor, the gravity amplifiers, and the gravity emitters.

The reactor

The reactor is the aircraft's primary power source, and it is encased inside a half-sphere-shaped component mounted on a metallic plate. Once the half-sphere is lifted, the reactor, which is shaped like a small cylindrical tower, is exposed. On the top of this tower, a triangular component is placed. This component is element 115, which is an element that does not appear naturally on Earth. When element 115 is placed on the reactor, gravitational waves are produced, and when exposed to radiation, a gravitational field is generated, allowing the aircraft to lift and propel.

The gravity amplifiers

Once the gravitational field is produced in the reactor, the gravity amplifiers amplify the gravitational wave, and the waves are then emitted through three large cylindrical devices, the gravity emitters.

The gravity emitters

The gravity emitters are able to rotate at 180 or 360 degrees, allowing the aircraft to either hover or propel forward. As the gravitational field increases, the gravitational waves surround the aircraft, allowing it to bend light, creating a distortion (this is what causes the cloaking effect). Consequently, as the gravitational field surrounds the aircraft, it distorts space-time and the aircraft is able to travel great distances in vastly shorter periods of time.

Credibility

The main reason I mention Bob Lazar's story is because it is extremely credible. His story has remained consistent over the years, and while he has been mocked by many, the information that has been recently released matches exactly the details he mentioned in 1989. First, Bob mentioned the existence of element 115 in 1989, back when element 115 had not yet even been discovered. It was only in 2003 that it was synthesized for the first time; the synthetic element is known to be extremely radioactive and has a half-life of just 0.65 seconds. Over a decade later, in 2015, a research team at the Lawrence Berkeley National Laboratory officially recognized element 115 as one of the new four elements.[8]

---

[8] Yu Ts Oganessian and V K Utyonkov, "Super-Heavy Element Research", Reports on Progress in Physics 78, 3 (2015).

A second corroborating factor is the existence of the S-4 facility. In 1989, nobody had even heard of S-4 or Area 51. In fact, it was because of Bob and his story that people became aware of the test range facility. George Knapp wanted to confirm Lazar's credibility and whether S-4 truly existed or not, so he phoned Nellis Air Force Base, who confirmed that the facility did exist, but they did not disclose its purpose. The last corroborating factor which I shall explore is the test flights. In his interviews, Lazar claimed that test flights were conducted on a specific weekday and at a specific time over Papoose Lake, which is located fifteen miles south of Area 51, just where he claimed S-4 was located. On three separate occasions, on the day and time Lazar specified, he and a group of his friends went to a nearby mountain ridge and observed strange lights in the sky, even capturing them on film. Naturally, he could only have known these details if he had truly worked there himself. On the third occasion, however, Lazar and his friends were apprehended.

From thereon, his safety was jeopardized; his house was broken into several times, but not by burglars as nothing was ever stolen. To intimidate and scare him, the intruders moved furniture around. On numerous occasions, Lazar would even find his car doors open, and on one occasion a pistol was placed on his car seat. It was because of these mind games and because Lazar started fearing for his life and safety that he contacted George Knapp to tell all he knew about what was happening over at S-4.[9,10] For a more detailed account on Lazar and his story, I highly recommend his autobiographical memoir, *Dreamland*, and the documentary *Bob Lazar: Area 51 & Flying Saucers*, directed by Jeremy Corbell.

▲ ▼ ▲

I believe that it is futile to explore the phenomenon of close encounters without first exploring the implications that come with it, and the implications explored in this chapter are just two of many. This book is divided into two parts and will explore some of the most fascinating and extraordinary phenomena and accounts. As we explore the following cases, I encourage you to approach them with an open mind and to

---

[9] Bob Lazar, *Dreamland: An Autobiography* (Interstellar, 2019).
[10] Jeremy Corbell, *Bob Lazar: Area 51 & Flying Saucers*, 2018.

remember that we are just one tiny speck of life sharing the universe with other intelligent and more advanced life-forms. We may not know what their intentions are or why they are so intrigued by us and our planet. As Stanton Friedman once told me, they are here for their own purposes, not ours, and although we may not understand the phenomenon completely, we must acknowledge that they exist and that they are here.

HYNEK'S UFO CLASSIFICATION SCALE

Dr. J. Allen Hynek, a well-known astronomer and UFO researcher, served as an advisor to the Air Force on several projects that investigated UFO cases, including Projects Sign, Grudge, and Blue Book. Throughout his decades of research, Hynek proposed a scale which categorizes UFO sightings according to the magnitude and detail of the encounter, as well as the observer's proximity to the aircraft.

Level 1: Nocturnal lights

The first level includes UFO reports which are typically made at night and involve the observer seeing bright lights in the sky. These are the most common type of UFO reports, and the detail is very minute since the observer is not in close proximity to the aircraft. The general description usually consists of "bright glows" or "balls of light."

Level 2: Daylight discs

The second level includes reports which are made in the daytime. The observer generally describes the unidentified aircraft as having unconventional characteristics, such as a disk or cigar shape, lacking an

xxvi   HYNEK'S UFO CLASSIFICATION SCALE

exhaust plume and a visible propulsion system. The aircraft's maneuverability is also unconventional; many witnesses have described
UFOs to move erratically and effortlessly, before disappearing in an
instant.

It is important to note that the majority of UFO sightings tend to be
misidentifications of military aircraft, satellites, or simply natural phenomena. For this reason, there are five distinguishing characteristics
that, when present, indicate that the unidentified aircraft is of extraterrestrial origin. With the technology we currently have, it is virtually
impossible for terrestrial aircraft to possess any of these five observables. The more observables an aircraft possesses, the more likely it is to
be of extraterrestrial origin.

Observable #1: Anti-gravity propulsion system

Every terrestrial aircraft has a visible means of propulsion, which produces exhaust. The majority of UAP, on the other hand, do not have a
visible propulsion system nor any other flight characteristics, such as
wings. These aircraft overcome Earth's gravity by generating their own
gravitational field, allowing them to hover and propel.

Observable #2: Instantaneous acceleration

Many witnesses describe how UFOs perform erratic maneuvers and
instantaneous accelerations. They appear and then vanish in an instant.
These aircraft defy the laws of physics and aerodynamics and travel
at speeds that no human being could possibly withstand. The g-forces
produced are simply insurmountable.

Observable #3: Hypersonic velocity

Any aircraft which exceeds the speed of sound produces what is
known as a sonic boom. Military pilots who have pursued UFOs
and tracked them on radar have stated that these aircraft travel at
incredible speeds and break the sound barrier without producing a
sonic boom. Since sound travels through a medium, one of the few
explanations of this anomaly could be that UAP travel through a vac-
uum, in non-matter. This idea corroborates the first observable, that

extraterrestrial aircraft operate by using an anti-gravitational propulsion system.

Observable #4: Trans-medium travel

These advanced aircraft also have the capability of travelling across different mediums, such as outer space, the atmosphere, and under water. Military pilots such as Commander Fravor have witnessed UFOs travelling at incredible speeds before plummeting into the ocean, only to resurface and continue to outperform their fighter jet.

Observable #5: Cloaking effect

The fifth observable is the cloaking effect—the aircraft's ability to reduce its visibility by creating a distortion. This distortion is presumably created by the gravitational field which surrounds the aircraft. It is because of this cloaking effect that many UFOs are described as appearing hazy and the observers are unable to discern the aircraft's features.

Level 3: Radar-visual

The third level includes cases in which the UAP is seen visually and is also tracked on radar. Radar sightings are significant because they provide concrete evidence of the UFO's existence, which immediately strengthens a case's credibility.

Level 4: Close encounters of the first kind

Close encounters of the first kind refer to reports made by individuals who were in close proximity to the UFO, and thus include great detail since the observer can easily discern its characteristics.

Level 5: Close encounters of the second kind

Close encounters of the second kind refer to cases in which the individual is in close proximity to the aircraft and following the encounter, they experienced immediate and intermediate aftereffects. These effects will be discussed at great length later in the book, but they generally include physiological and psychological symptoms.

Level 6: Close encounters of the third kind

Close encounters of the third kind refer to cases in which the individual is in extreme close proximity to the aircraft and witnesses the presence of an extraterrestrial entity. The being's strange and absurd characteristics immediately indicate that they are of extraterrestrial origin.

Level 7: Close encounters of the fourth kind

Close encounters of the fourth kind include cases in which the individual is abducted by an extraterrestrial entity.

PART 1

CLOSE ENCOUNTERS
OF THE THIRD KIND

CHAPTER 1

Introduction

C lose encounters of the third kind refer to UFO reports in which the individual is in close proximity to the aircraft and witnesses the presence of an extraterrestrial entity. This phenomenon, just like the UFO phenomenon, occurs on a global scale, with reports coming in from all over the world. In the majority of cases, the aircraft's unconventional characteristics as well as the being's obscure details immediately indicate that they are of extraterrestrial origin. As we shall see in the coming chapters, although these cases are fascinating and engrossing, they can also be quite traumatic. The cases I chose to include in this book are among the most compelling and include evidence which cannot be easily refuted. These cases prove that extraterrestrial entities exist ... but leave unanswered what is the reason behind these visitations?

CHAPTER 2

"Attacked by a spaceship"

Date: 9th November 1979
Location: Dechmont Law, Scotland

Robert Taylor had spent a number of years serving in the army; when the war broke out in 1939, he joined the Fife and Forfar Yeomanry and fought in the Battle of Normandy and also took part in the evacuation from Dunkirk. In 1944 Taylor returned to his homeland, Scotland, to live a more peaceful and serene life. His days in Scotland were antithetical to the army days—instead of experiencing the thrill and ferocity of war, he now worked as a forester in Livingston. The 9th of November 1979 began as an ordinary day, but as the day unfolded, he would experience a phenomenal encounter that was nothing short of extraordinary. This is Robert Taylor's close encounter.

The encounter
9th November 1979

It was a Friday morning in Livingston, Scotland, and sixty-year-old Robert Taylor was to go to the hillside known as Dechmont Law to carry out his forestry duties. With him to work, Robert often brought his Irish red setter Lara, and the two arrived at the site at around 10:20. The day was as routine as any other, Robert's task being to ensure there were no stray sheep in the area. As Robert and Lara walked through the hillside, they reached a clearing, and it was at that moment that Robert's transformative experience would begin. In the middle of the clearing among the trees was a sight he would never forget: a disk-shaped aircraft hovering just a few feet above the ground.

The aircraft had a silver metallic surface and was roughly twenty foot in diameter with a dome structure on its top. Around its circumference were antenna-looking spikes and equidistant portholes. The disk simply hovered, completely silently, as Taylor stood in disbelief, unaware of what he was seeing before his very eyes. After a few seconds, the sight became even more bizarre when the disk became translucent. The aircraft had completely dematerialized, and the surrounding trees in the background that the disk had been obstructing became visible ... the disk had vanished completely. Shortly thereafter the disk re-materialized once again. At that moment, Taylor's mind was racing with questions; first, what aircraft could possess such peculiar characteristics? Second, where did it come from?

Unbeknown to Taylor, this was only the beginning of the encounter. As the disk re-materialized, two spheres dropped from beneath it and started rolling rapidly towards his position. Aside from the differing shape and size, the spheres had similar characteristics to the disk: they were around five feet in diameter and had the same silver color. They also had the same rough, metallic texture with spikes spread over the surface. Once the two spheres reached Taylor's position, they attached to his legs and it was at that moment he felt a sharp, piercing pain. With the two spheres now attached to Taylor's sides, he dropped to the ground and was dragged towards the aircraft. He also became aware of a foul taste in his mouth and a nauseating odor which he compared to burning brake linings. These sensations were the last things Taylor could recall before losing consciousness.

After twenty minutes, Taylor slowly began to regain consciousness; he was on the ground as Lara desperately tugged on his shirt, trying to wake him up. As he awoke, he felt a pulsing headache, a burning sensation on his chin and a dryness in his mouth. He attempted to stand up but felt too lethargic. His truck was close by, and he had no other choice but to crawl to the vehicle to call for help. As he reached the truck, he noticed that it was stuck in a ditch, and adding to the situation, the radio communicating system had malfunctioned and he was thus unable to use it, leaving him completely stranded. Luckily, Dechmont Law was just a mile and a half away from his home, so the only option he had left was to walk it back. After he regained some energy, he staggered across the field and eventually made his way back to the house.

As he walked through the front door, Mary, Robert's wife, was shocked to see him in such a horrible state. His clothes were covered in mud, his trousers were torn, and he had a graze under his chin. Mary bombarded him with questions and was convinced that he had been assaulted, but Robert kept reiterating that he had been "attacked by a spaceship."[11] Naturally she did not believe or accept such a ludicrous explanation, but despite her persistence, Robert kept insisting that he was indeed telling the truth. Regardless of what happened, he needed to be seen by a doctor, and so his wife phoned their family doctor, Gordon Adams as well as his boss, Malcolm Drummond. As the two arrived at the house, Taylor related his encounter from the start. He described how the disk-shaped aircraft just appeared in the middle of the clearing and then proceeded to de-materialize. Taylor's voice trembled as he went on to describe how the two spheres attached to his leg and dragged his body towards the disk. At that moment, his wife realized that he would not have made up such a preposterous story. It was undeniably an outrageous account, but those who knew Robert knew that he was not one to come up with such tales.

At the house, Dr. Adams examined Robert and noted the graze under his chin. He took note of his blood pressure, which was normal, and from his assessment it did not seem that he was suffering from any head injuries. With that being said, he still advised him to go to the hospital for a full and thorough examination. Robert did agree to go, but after spending several hours waiting to be seen, he signed himself out and returned back home.

---

[11] "UFOs," *Arthur C. Clarke's Mysterious World* (ITV Network, November 4, 1980).

The investigation

While Taylor waited at the hospital, his boss Malcolm and some of his colleagues visited the site at Dechmont Law to try to locate any physical markings. They were unable to find any impressions on the ground, but when they informed Robert of this, he was adamant that they had simply not located the precise location and insisted that he goes with them. This time round, Robert found the location and was relieved to find physical markings to corroborate his story.

> In the center were something like caterpillar tracks, surrounded by deep triangular marks, the size of a horse's hoof. There is no doubt in my mind that these marks were made by a perfectly solid heavier-than-air object. They had been made by some machine which had come vertically down.[12]

The tracks in the center were similar to *caterpillar tracks*, and surrounding it were deep triangular marks. Interestingly, the markings were located solely in the center of the area—they did not lead to or from anywhere, which means that the vehicle or aircraft that left the markings had made a vertical descent and ascent. To preserve the markings the men fenced off the area and took photographs, and after some encouragement, they managed to convince Robert to file an official police report.

Detective Constable Ian Walk was one of the first officers on the scene and immediately took note of the two parallel landing marks. The constable took photographs and measurements; he noted that the landing marks were each ten foot long, a foot wide and seven foot apart. He also noticed how these tracks were surrounded by several other round depressions that penetrated the ground at a slight angle and were four inches deep.

> Mr. Taylor is a respected member of the community and is described as a conscientious and trustworthy person, not likely to invent such a story.[13]

---

[12] Malcolm Robinson, *The Dechmont Woods UFO Incident (An Ordinary Day, An Extraordinary Event)* (Lulu.com, 2019, pp. 17–18).
[13] Robinson, *The Dechmont Woods UFO Incident*, p. 58.

The forensic analysis

As part of the police investigation, Taylor's clothes were sent for forensic analysis and the findings further corroborated Taylor's testimony. The analysis confirmed that the tears were not caused by burning and indicated that Taylor had been pulled upwards. The official report reads as follows:

> The police scientist who examined the trousers determined that neither the tears nor the holes were caused by burning. But he was sure that the tears could only have been caused by a strong mechanical pull upwards, or by the person wearing them jumping downwards and catching his trousers on projections.[14]

The analysis further noted the mud smears on the front of his pullover and two tears on his trousers at the hip region. On the left side of the trousers were three tears: a three-inch horizontal tear that connected to two other vertical tears, one an inch long and the other half an inch long. The right side of the trousers had corresponding tears: an inch-long horizontal tear connected to two vertical tears, both being two inches long. An "S" shaped tear on the left side of the trousers was also discovered, indicating the motion of being grabbed and lifted from the ground.

Up until this point, the only people who knew of Robert's encounter were a few of his colleagues, but a few days later, *The Livingston Post* was informed of the incident, allegedly by someone claiming to be Taylor's colleague. From then on, word continued to spread, and many media personnel and investigators made their way to Livingston to speak with Robert. Two of these individuals were Andrew Collings (from BUFORA—the British UFO Research Association) and Martin Keatman (from the UFO Investigators Network). The two investigators asked to go to the landing site, and although Taylor's colleagues had fenced it off, it was evident that the area had been trespassed and the landing marks had been walked over. Despite this, the markings were still visible, and they measured and photographed the two parallel

---

[14] Steuart Campbell, "Close Encounter in Scotland," *Journal of Transient Aerial Phenomena*, 1(2) (1979).

markings as well as the surrounding spherical depressions. They also noted that the ground had not been pierced, but that the depressions were caused by the heavy weight of the objects.

A month had now passed, and Robert's encounter was still being covered extensively by the press. Throughout all of the interviews Taylor's viewpoint remained unchanged: he firmly believed that the aircraft he witnessed was extraterrestrial in origin. In December of the same year, Taylor was interviewed by a psychologist, Graham Philips, who confirmed that he was of sound mental health. He even underwent hypnotic regression, but his narrative remained unchanged and did not provide any further details.

▲ ▼ ▲

Hypotheses

More than four decades have passed since Taylor's encounter at Dechmont Law, and many individuals have proposed different hypotheses to explain his encounter with the unknown. Before we explore the hypotheses, it is important to remain mindful of the aforementioned evidence: the landing marks and the forensic analysis carried out on Taylor's clothes.

Hypothesis #1: A stroke

The first hypothesis we shall explore suggests that Taylor suffered a stroke or a transient ischemic attack (a mini-stroke). The physiological symptoms Taylor experienced (the headache, dry mouth, lethargy, and loss of consciousness) are indeed symptoms of a stroke, but this hypothesis does not account for the tears in his clothes or the presence of the landing marks which support the idea that there was indeed a vehicle or object of some sort at the site. Furthermore, following this incident, Robert recuperated without any complications, which would have been quite atypical if he had indeed suffered a stroke.

Hypothesis #2: A seizure

The second hypothesis was postulated by Steuart Campbell, and admittedly, it is somewhat far-fetched. Campbell suggests that as Taylor was walking through the woods, he observed a bright Venus in the sky which caused him to suffer a seizure. Campbell further argues that the physical symptoms Taylor experienced were congruent with that of a seizure, and the disk he reported seeing was merely a hallucination. In regard to the landing marks, Campbell states that they were caused by machinery which was left lain in the middle of the field, whereas the tears on the clothing had been there prior to the incident but had simply gone unnoticed.

> … stimulus for the epileptic seizure was the shock of seeing the sudden appearance of the bright and strange mirage. If the approach of the "spheres" was accompanied by a strong smell (indicating that Taylor had already entered the aura phase), then his account of events at that point, and from then on, may be based on a hallucination.[15]

This hypothesis is illogical for several reasons, but first, how many people who have had seizures have reported seeing a disk-shaped aircraft and were dragged by metallic spheres? I presume that the number is not very high. However, let us put this aside and dissect the hypothesis nonetheless. How possible is it for Taylor to have spotted a bright Venus in broad daylight, causing him to have a seizure? It is difficult to locate Venus in broad daylight, but even if you know exactly where to look at in the sky, the chances of suffering a seizure due to its brightness are extremely unlikely. While I admire the creativity involved to come up with such a perfect scenario, I do believe that this hypothesis does not sufficiently explain Taylor's encounter.

> Taylor was startled by a mirage of Venus (with or without the participation of other astronomical objects) which sent him into an epileptic fit. The ground marks and torn trousers have no connection with Taylor's visual experience.[16]

Hypothesis #3: The extraterrestrial hypothesis

The third hypothesis we shall explore is the extraterrestrial hypothesis, meaning that Taylor provided a truthful account of what happened, and the encounter was indeed a close encounter with an extraterrestrial

---

[15] Steuart Campbell, "Livingston: A New Hypothesis", *Journal of Transient Aerial Phenomena*, 4(3) (1986).
[16] Ibid.

aircraft. The factors which support this theory include the physical evidence as well as the tears found on Taylor's clothes. If we look at the physical markings, the fact that they were only in the center of the clearing indicates that they were created by a hovering aircraft. Additionally, the other spherical depressions further support Taylor's testimony. Aside from the physical markings, the forensic analysis carried out on his clothing also corroborate Robert's narrative. The analysis confirmed that Robert must have been grabbed and pulled upwards, just as he had stated. Is it possible that Robert fabricated the entire story? Yes, it is possible, but those close to him have stated that it would have been completely out of character. Moreover, out of all the theories we have explored, the extraterrestrial hypothesis is the only one which sufficiently provides an explanation for every factor and detail of the encounter. With that being said, is this enough to conclude that this was indeed an otherworldly encounter?

Conclusion

From 1979 throughout the remainder of his life, Robert remained consistent with his story and reiterated that the aircraft he had seen in the woods was extraterrestrial in origin. Naturally, the concept of Taylor having encountered an extraterrestrial aircraft is difficult to comprehend. When we are faced with the idea that an ordinary individual experienced something as unexplainable and inconceivable as this, the easiest thing to do is to disregard the evidence and deride the individual and their testimony.

Everyone will have their own opinion, and in a way, this opinion is shaped by preconceived ideas and biases. With that being said it is important that we challenge these biases with the facts and evidence. In this case, the evidence includes the landing marks and the clothes analysis. We must take these factors into account, and it is only then that we can come to an informed opinion on what happened in the Dechmont woods in 1979.

> I have no doubt that something landed there. What it was I have no idea. Forty years on, it still hasn't been solved. (Detective Constable Ian Walk)[17]

---

[17] *The One Show* (BBC, February 26, 2020).

CHAPTER 3

The Falcon Lake incident

Date: 20th May 1967
Location: Falcon Lake, Canada

Stefan Michalak and his family were Polish natives who had been living in Winnipeg, Canada, for more than a decade after fleeing their
war-torn homeland following World War II. Together with his wife and
three children, Michalak led a quiet and modest lifestyle; he worked as
an industrial mechanic during the day and frequently went on prospecting expeditions in search of minerals during his free time. In the
spring of 1967, Stefan planned a quick weekend getaway to the idyllic
Whiteshell Provincial Park as it was a promising location for prospecting. What was supposed to be a peaceful break from his daily routine
turned out to be an unexpected encounter with an unidentified aircraft.
Several years later, Michalak would continue to suffer from ailments
related to this encounter. This is Stefan Michalak's close encounter of
the third kind.

The encounter
20th May 1967

It was Saturday the 20th of May and Michalak had planned a quick weekend getaway for himself at Whiteshell Provincial Park in Falcon Lake. Michalak was eager to go prospecting in the enchanting forest after a typical workweek. That morning, he woke up early at 05:30, prepared some lunch, packed his equipment, and set out from his house in Winnipeg. Upon his arrival at the park, Michalak started prospecting for minerals, and the day continued on as planned. At around 11:00, he found a quiet area and ate his lunch as he watched a flock of geese pass by. Around an hour later, he continued on his journey through the park. It was the ideal spot for prospecting, as he had been able to locate several minerals along the trail. The flock of geese he had had seen a while ago were still visible, although he now noticed that they appeared to be agitated. He didn't think too much into this, although as we shall subsequently see, this sight portended the perplexing encounter he was about to experience.

As Michalak continued to walk along the trail, his attention was suddenly caught by two strange aircraft flying overhead: they were both disk-shaped with a diameter of around forty feet, had a silver, smooth, metallic surface and a dome-shaped structure on top. The aircraft's features became more visible as the sun reflected off their metallic surface, and Michalak was immediately perplexed by the salient features. The disks began to slowly descend toward the ground as Michalak looked ahead, startled by the sight. While one of the disks sped off into the distance at an insurmountable speed, the other one made a smooth landing on the ground, just a few feet away from him. Though the disk exhibited many of the characteristics commonly associated with UFOs, the thought of it originating from another planet did not cross his mind … at least not at first. Surrounding the circumference were numerous, equally spaced portholes, and its gleaming metallic surface alternated from glowing bright red to striking stainless steel. The forty-foot disk did not have any discernable insignia etched on its smooth surface, and it also lacked wings or any other flight characteristics, which added to Michalak's confusion.

From the inside of the aircraft Michalak could hear a mechanical noise of some sort, and he presumed that this was a military aircraft and the personnel inside were experiencing some trouble. After a few minutes,

Michalak decided to approach the aircraft and try to communicate with the people inside. As he approached the disk, he noticed a small rectangular feature on its exterior that he assumed was a vent as it was wafting warm air from the inside. Michalak started shouting, asking the people inside if they needed help. As he did not get a reply, he moved even closer to the disk and asked once more, this time in Russian, German, French, Italian, and Ukrainian, in hopes that the people inside spoke one of the languages. Alas he did not receive a reply.

He inched even closer, and a hatch suddenly appeared in the disk's center, and as it opened, a blinding violet light emanated from the inside. Michalak caught a glimpse of the interior, but the piercing light blinded him and prevented him from getting a good look. He did however notice that the walls were extremely thick, about twenty inches thick, and the hatch closed after a few seconds.

> When Mr. A turned his attention to the landed craft, it, too was changing color from glowing red to the iridescence of hot stainless steel. The craft had no markings. Intense purple light shone from apertures around the dome of the craft. Mr. A noticed watts of warm air, a smell of sulphur, and a hissing sound from the craft. He sketched the object. After about 15 min. he noticed that a hatch on the side of the craft had opened. He could see nothing inside, because the light was too bright.[18]

At that moment, Michalak was wearing his protective gloves, and he touched the disk's surface to get a better feel of it. Although the gloves were heat-resistant, the moment he touched the surface they started to melt. He then started hearing a faint whooshing noise, and the aircraft slowly started ascending from the ground at a slight tilt. Michalak was standing just a few feet away, and a blast of warm air from the rectangular vent hit his body, making him fall to the ground. The heat was scorching to the point that his clothes caught fire. He quickly undressed himself and stomped on them. At that point, the disk was several feet in the air and after a few moments it accelerated rapidly out of sight.

---

[18] Edward Condon, *Scientific Study of Unidentified Flying Objects*, ed. Daniel Gillmor (Bantam Books, 1969), Case 22.

He was left with burns on his abdomen and sickened, apparently as a result of inhalation of vapors from the machine. Mr. A said he suffered headache, nausea and cold sweats within minutes after the experience.

Now that the disk had disappeared out of sight, Michalak felt relieved, but was experiencing an excruciating pain all over his body. He walked back to where he had left his equipment, gathered his belongings and what remained of the burnt shirt and undershirt. He required immediate medical attention, but he was also stranded in the middle of the park, so he had to walk back to the motel which he had planned to stay at for the duration of the trip. Aside from the burn marks all over his body, he started seeing bright pink dots. He also had a very dry mouth and could smell a strong sulfuric odor which made him extremely nauseous, causing him to vomit. As he was walking back towards the motel, staggering along the highway, he encountered a constable of the Royal Canadian Mounted Police (RCMP), and he hoped that the officer would assist him. Michalak looked disheveled and was incoherent, and thus the officer dismissed him altogether (in his witness statement, the RCMP constable confirmed that Michalak did not appear intoxicated and did not smell of alcohol).

Michalak continued walking, having to stop several times along the way to vomit. After the grueling walk, upon his arrival at the motel he was informed that the nearest doctor was several miles away. He did not want to call back home and alarm his family, but he was also unable to reach the doctor by himself. Michalak was desperate, and in a panic, he tried to think of a way to get medical attention as soon as possible. He surmised that if a news outlet learned about his incident, they would immediately dispatch a doctor to verify his claims, so he frantically called *The Winnipeg Tribune*, but they, too, dismissed his story. Having no other option, Michalak phoned back home and was collected by his wife and son shortly thereafter. His family were shocked at his condition and rushed him to a doctor. Michalak knew that no one, especially a medical professional, would believe him if he claimed to have seen a flying saucer. Thus, when the doctor inquired about the burn marks, Michalak explained how he had been hit by the exhaust of a plane which was flying at a low altitude. The explanation seemed to suffice, and he left the doctor's office with anti-nausea medication, painkillers, and a sedative to help with the shock.

Several hours had now passed but the pain did not subside. The following day his pain had actually worsened, and he could not keep any food or liquid down. Michalak's condition worried his wife, who phoned their family doctor, Dr. Oatway. The doctor drove to the Michalak household to assess him and prescribed anti-bacterial cleanser for the burns and concluded that the symptoms he was experiencing were akin to radiation exposure. This warranted an immediate intervention and it was recommended that he go to the National Atomic Research Center. The doctors there confirmed that his burns were thermal and did not have a high radioactive reading.

▲ ▼ ▲

The investigation

The RCMP initiated an investigation on the 24th of May, four days after the incident. After taking Michalak's witness statement they accompanied him back to Falcon Lake to identify the landing site. The investigation and situation were tense from the start; a number of people had accompanied Michalak and the constables to Falcon Lake, and while Michalak struggled to remember the trail, many people kept interfering with their suggestions for the path of travel. Unable to locate the landing site, the RCMP dismissed the case and investigation altogether. In their official report, the RCMP included the fact that everyone's interference had affected Michalak's ability to recall the location of the site.

> Michalak stated that he felt the main reason he could not find the right place during his previous attempts was because too many people were involved and were suggesting various places for him to look at. He said that he felt that if he had been left to look and follow the rock formation on his own without inference from others, he would have found it earlier.[19]

---

[19] Royal Canadian Mounted Police, "Stefan Michalak—Report of Unidentified Flying Object, Falcon Beach, Manitoba. 20 May 67," Library and Archives Canada, 1967, https://bac-lac.gc.ca/eng/discover/unusual/ufo/Documents/1967-08-10.pdf.

At this point, days turned into weeks and Michalak's body still ached and was still covered in burn marks. His condition kept deteriorating and he was rapidly losing weight; blood tests showed that his lymphocyte count had alarmingly dropped from twenty-five percent to sixteen percent. His constant headaches and nausea persisted, and a rash developed over his chest and neck. Adding to his pain and discomfort was the frustration at the authorities who had completely dismissed the investigation. Not only did he not have answers to his physical ailments, but also as to what the aircraft was or where it had originated from.

A month had now passed and Michalak knew that the only way he was going to get answers was to conduct an investigation himself. Together with Gerald Hart, an electronic engineer, Michalak returned to the Whiteshell park on the 23rd of June. This time, Michalak took his time, and without the interference and pressure from others, was able to successfully locate the landing site. The impressions on the ground were still visible: aside from the outline of the disk embedded in the ground, contrasting the branches and vegetation nearby were the withered branches which surrounded the landing site. Michalak now felt relieved that there was another eyewitness as well as physical evidence to prove his narrative. The two men collected some earth samples and hurried back to the RCMP in Winnipeg, where they informed the constables of their findings and handed in the samples. At the station, they spoke with Squadron Leader Bissiky, who accompanied the men back to the landing site. The officers identified the location, measured and photographed the depressions, and collected their own samples.

Radiation levels

Corroborating Michalak's statements and the impressions on the ground was the high radiation reading in the area. The reading was substantial enough for the Safety Assessment and Control Section to be informed of the situation. As the following excerpt from the official memorandum states, the findings do not conclude what the aircraft was or whether it was extraterrestrial or not as that was not the scope of the document. It does however confirm that the soil samples and the area had a high radioactive reading which was deemed a hazard to the general public.

The undersigned does not intend to prove one way or another whether a UFO had been sighted as there are still too many unknowns. Secondly, in the opinion of the writer such ventures are outside the main interests of this Division.

There are however two conclusions that are of interest to this Division, they are as follows:

a) Radioactive contamination of rock and lichens was found at the alleged UFO landing site. The origin of this contamination has yet to be determined.

b) The radiation levels measured were not high enough to create a radiation hazard to the general public.[20]

The officers also collected numerous earth samples from the area; some from the landing site and some from the surroundings to be used as a control sample. The findings of the analysis were intriguing and note-worthy: the rock, soil, and vegetation from the landing site all contained a higher than average radiation reading. The following is an extract from the official RCMP report dated the 10th of August 1967:

Laboratory tests here indicate earth samples taken from scene highly radioactive. Radiation Protection Division of Department of Health and Welfare concerned that others may be exposed if travel in area not restricted. Suggest you close off area completely.[21]

The remnants of Michalak's burned shirt and the measuring tape also had a high radiation reading.

Soil sample, steel tape and burned clothing obtained from Defense Research Board Lab Ottawa 18 Jul 67. Tape also radioactive.[22]

[20] S. E. Hunt (Department of Health and Welfare), "Determination of Possible Radiation Hazards to the General Public from the Alleged Landing Site of an Unidentified Flying Object near Falcon Lake, Manitoba," Library and Archives Canada, September 1967, https://bac-lac.gc.ca/eng/discover/unusual/ufo/Documents/1967-09-13.pdf.
[21] Royal Canadian Mounted Police, "Stefan Michalak—Report of Unidentified Flying Object, Falcon Beach, Manitoba. 20 May 67," Library and Archives Canada, 1967, https://bac-lac.gc.ca/eng/discover/unusual/ufo/Documents/1967-08-10.pdf.
[22] Ibid.

The aftermath

Weeks and months had now passed and Michalak was still riddled with pain and discomfort. Having said that, he did not have the financial means to stay at home, so he returned to work on the 21st of September. Michalak was pushing his body to its limits, and a few hours into the workday he started experiencing a severe burning sensation around his neck and chest, prompting him to rush to the first aid room. His superior followed him and saw that his body started to swell up and red spots were forming over his body, which was now turning purple. His vision also started to fade, and he was quickly rushed to the Misericordia Hospital where he was stabilized. The doctors discharged him the following day, attributing his symptoms to an allergic reaction, although they did not specify to what the allergic reaction had been.

After a year, Michalak was still experiencing health problems, and the burn marks had still not faded either. Apart from the frustration Michalak experienced from the investigation, what aggravated him further was the fact that no medical professional was able to explain to him what was causing the physical ailments. Desperate for answers, he visited the Mayo Clinic and was also assessed by a psychiatrist who reassured him that he was not suffering from any psychiatric illnesses. A full body examination was performed, but this is where things got even more bizarre. After his assessments, several weeks passed by and he did not receive the results or answers from the clinic. However, he continued to receive the bills which he paid in full. When he finally decided to call the clinic to inquire about the results, they informed him that they did not have a Stefan Michalak in their system, even though Michalak had records of the paperwork, bills, and the clinic's outpatient identity card. His file had somehow been erased from the system. Was this mishap done on purpose or was it simply an accident? What is odd, however, is the fact that they kept insisting that he had never visited the clinic, despite having all the paperwork to prove so.

The Condon investigation

If Mr. A's reported experience were physically real, it would show the existence of alien flying vehicles in our environment.[23]

---

[23] Condon, *Final Report of the Scientific Study of Unidentified Flying Objects*, Case 22.

Michalak's encounter was one of the cases which was investigated by the Condon Committee, the UFO study funded by the United States Air Force between 1966 and 1968. Those who are familiar with the Condon Report are aware that the majority of the conclusions they provided were nothing short of ludicrous. A perfect example would be Michalak's case; the Committee speculated that Michalak's burn marks could have been caused by an insect bite. This theory is incongruent with the physical symptoms Michalak experienced as well as the explanations the medical professionals provided; that the burn marks were thermal.

Following the encounter, Michalak often returned to the landing site with a Geiger counter to document the radiation readings, and on one occasion, a year after the encounter, he made an odd discovery; buried two inches beneath a layer of lichen he discovered two metallic fragments in the shape of a "W" which were just about four inches long. He also located smaller pieces of irregularly shaped metallic fragments. It is important to note that Michalak never claimed that these fragments were related to his experience, but he handed them over to the officials nonetheless.

> This material reportedly consisted of two W-shaped bars of metal, each about 4.5 inches long, and several smaller pieces of irregular shape. These items were said to have been found about 2 inches below a layer of lichen in the rock fissure ... In view of the thoroughness of earlier searches of the site for radioactive material, it is improbable that the particles discovered a year later would have been missed had they been present when the earlier searches were made.[24]

Many individuals and skeptics have used this finding to tarnish Michalak's integrity by stating that he planted the fragments himself. However, this is not the case; Michalak never claimed that these metallic fragments were of extraterrestrial origin, nor did he claim that they were linked to his encounter. They very well could have been planted there by someone else, or they could have been a purely coincidental and insignificant discovery.

---

[24] Condon, *Final Report of the Scientific Study of Unidentified Flying Objects*, Case 22.

Hypotheses

Hypothesis #1: The extraterrestrial hypothesis

The first hypothesis we shall explore is the extraterrestrial hypothesis, which may be the theory we have the most evidence for. The factors which support this theory are: a) Michalak's rapid health deterioration, b) the landing marks, c) the radiation levels, d) the constable's testimony, and lastly, e) Michalak's intentions.

The biggest mystery of this case is the rapid and drastic deterioration in Michalak's health, which he continued to suffer from for several months after the incident. Although the doctors stated that they were only first-degree burn marks, they did not fade, despite the treatment. Furthermore, the blood analysis showed that his lymphocyte count dropped from twenty-five percent to sixteen percent. Other ailments he suffered from were rapid weight loss, persistent nausea, and problems with his vision. The tests revealed that he was not suffering from a previously unknown illness, thus the only plausible explanation is that this was caused by his interaction with the aircraft. As part of AAWSA, the Defense of Intelligence explored injuries associated with UAP encounters, and the immediate and intermediate effects listed are congruent with Michalak's symptoms.

The next corroborative factors are the landing marks at the site and the high radiation readings. The disk left a discernible impression of its outline on the ground, and the surrounding branches and vegetation had all withered. Aside from that, the site had a higher than average radiation reading; this was also discovered in the soil sample and the remnants of Michalak's clothing and tape measure. Michalak's genuineness and authenticity is another important factor which we must examine. Skeptics have long speculated that Michalak was intoxicated; however, this can be debated. The constable who encountered Michalak on the highway stated that he did not smell the odor of liquor on him. Naturally, his appearance did seem disheveled, but that is to be expected after such an incident.

> I could not smell the odor of liquor on Michalak. His general appearance was not dissimilar to that of a person who has over indulged. His eyes were bloodshot and when questioned in detail he could or would not answer coherently.[25]

---

[25] Royal Canadian Mounted Police, "Stefan Michalak—Report of Unidentified Flying Object, Falcon Beach, Manitoba. 20 May 67," Library and Archives Canada, 1967, https://bac lac.gc.ca/eng/discover/unusual/ufo/Documents/1967-06-18.pdf.

The last corroborating factor which supports the extraterrestrial hypothesis is Michalak's intentions. In the report published by the Condon Committee, they too noted that he is a sincere and genuine individual. Aside from that, Michalak never attempted to gain any fame or money from his encounter. He did publish a small booklet detailing his experience, but he did not profit from it (conversely, he lost money), and his rationale for doing so was to warn others in case they were to encounter a similar aircraft.

> Mr. A was deemed very reliable by his employer. He had convinced representatives of the RCMP and RCAF, two of the several physicians involved, as well as his family, that he was telling the story of a real event. During the project investigator's review, he seemed honest, sincere and concerned. His presentation of his story was convincing. His wife and son verified his claim of an unusual odor coming from his body after his alleged UFO experience, indicating that the odor permeated the bathroom after Mr. A had bathed.[26]

Hypothesis #2: A military aircraft

Is it possible that the aircraft he encountered was a military aircraft, perhaps part of a top-secret project? This is certainly possible; however, it is unlikely that the Air Force would have flown the aircraft over a public park. Test sites exist for a reason.

Hypothesis #3: A hoax

The final hypothesis we will investigate is the possibility that this case was a hoax. Skeptics support this hypothesis with two factors: the metallic fragments and the disk's flight path. As has been mentioned, Michalak discovered metallic fragments at the landing site several months after the incident, but he never claimed that they were linked to his encounter. With that being said, skeptics argue that he planted these fragments himself to corroborate his narrative. The second factor is the disk's flight path. In his witness statement, Michalak stated that he initially observed two disks: the first one accelerated rapidly out of sight while the other one made a smooth landing on the ground.

---

[26] Condon, *Final Report of the Scientific Study of Unidentified Flying Objects*, Case 22.

If the disk had sped away, skeptics argue that there would have been other eyewitnesses since it would have flown towards the direction of a nearby golf course. This is correct—if the aircraft had been traveling at a normal speed, it would have been possible for other individuals to spot it, but alas, it was not. For other witnesses to have seen the disk they would have had to look at a precise spot in the sky and at a very specific time. Even then, let us refer back to the five observables: UFOs have the ability to cloak themselves and travel at an insurmountable speed, making it highly improbable anyone would have been able to spot it.

Conclusion

Michalak's encounter with the unknown at Falcon Lake is one which leaves us with many unanswered questions. Was the aircraft of extraterrestrial origin or perhaps a top-secret military aircraft? Was it an accident that Michalak's medical records were lost, or were they intentionally erased? Although these questions may remain unanswered, we do have enough information to deduce that the aircraft Michalak encountered was certainly unconventional and caused a significant deterioration in his health. This case also demonstrates why this phenomenon is so important to study, as it emphasizes how little we know about these advanced aircraft and the consequences of coming into close contact with one.

CHAPTER 4

The Socorro landing

Date: 24th April 1964
Location: Socorro, New Mexico

It was the 24th of April 1964 at around 17:45. Lonnie Zamora, a sergeant police officer, was pursuing a reckless driver in Socorro, New Mexico, when he heard a loud roar that lasted at least ten seconds and saw a large, bluish-orange flame from a distance, right where a dynamite shack was located. Zamora assumed there must have been an explosion, and so he abandoned the car chase and immediately started driving toward the shack. As he drove to the top of the hill overlooking the shack, he witnessed a sight he would never forget, a sight which not even the Air Force would be able to explain. This is Lonnie Zamora's close encounter of the third kind.

The encounter
24th April 1964

As Zamora started driving towards the dynamite shack, he reached a hill which overlooked the shack. He was immediately puzzled by what he saw; he expected to see the aftermath of an explosion, but instead, from 200 yards away, he saw a shiny object with two figures standing alongside it. He then assumed that it was an overturned vehicle and that the people needed help, so he radioed the sheriff's office to inform him of this and asked for assistance. As he continued to drive closer to their position, Zamora then realized that this was not an accident after all, and the shiny object was certainly not a vehicle. In front him was a reflective, metallic, oval-shaped aircraft resting on two legs.

The aircraft had an unusually smooth surface with a red insignia etched on its center which is best described as an upward pointing arrow, with a horizontal line beneath it and an inverted "U" around it. Zamora sat in disbelief in the driver's seat as the two figures he had seen from afar came into clearer view; although he could not discern any unusual or distinguishable characteristics, from their size he assumed they were "small adults or large kids." Zamora continued to observe the aircraft and the beings, and at one point, as one of them noticed his presence, it became startled. This sighting only lasted for a couple of seconds; after noticing his presence, the being scurried away out of sight.

> Socorro 2 to Socorro, possible 10-44 (accident), I'll be 10-6 (busy) out of the car, checking the car down in the arroyo.[27]

At this point in the encounter Zamora was perplexed by what was happening. He exited the vehicle and started approaching their position when he heard a roar, which started off as a low frequency but gradually intensified and got louder. Simultaneously, from beneath the oval-shaped aircraft, a bluish-orange flame emerged, and it began an ascent toward the sky. Zamora was expecting an explosion to occur at any second, so he turned and started running back as fast as he could towards his vehicle. As he ran back, he bumped his leg on the car and fell to the ground, and from there he could see that the aircraft continued to ascend, now at twenty to twenty-five feet above the ground.

---

[27] Project Blue Book, National Archives—T-1206, Case 8766.

He quickly got up and radioed Ned Lopez, the radio operator, telling him to look out the window and keep an eye out for a large aircraft, but Lopez was unable to locate it. The aircraft was now picking up speed and was heading west in a straight trajectory, towards the Six Mile Canyon mountain, where it disappeared shortly thereafter.

▲ ▼ ▲

The investigation

Zamora was an esteemed officer and had no apparent reason to mount such a hoax, so an official investigation was initiated. That same afternoon, FBI Agent Arthur Byrnes Jr., who was stationed at Albuquerque, New Mexico and Army Captain Richard Holder spoke with Zamora and went to the landing site, where they observed the depressions and wrote up the following memorandum:

UNIDENTIFIED FLYING OBJECT
SOCORRO, NEW MEXICO
APRIL 24, 1964
Special Agent D. Arthur Byrnes, Jr., Federal Bureau of Investigation, stationed at Albuquerque, New Mexico was at Socorro, New Mexico, and at the State Police Office there on business late afternoon of April 24, 1964.

At approximately 5:45 to 5:50 P.M. [REDACTED] radio operator in the Socorro County Sheriff's Office, located about thirty feet down the hall from the State Police Office, came into the State Police Office.

[REDACTED] advised [REDACTED] New Mexico state Police, that he had just received a radio call from Officer Lonnie Zamora to come to an area about one mile southwest of Socorro. The call was in relation to some unknown object which "landed and has taken off." Agent Byrnes finished his work in the State Police Office at Socorro at approximately 6:00 P.M., April 24, 1964, thereafter proceeded to the site where Officer Zamora, Socorro Country Undersheriff [REDACTED], Sergeant [REDACTED] and Officer [REDACTED] New Mexico State Police, were assembled.

It may be noted that it has been the observation of Agent Byrnes that Officer Zamora, known intimately for approximately five years, is well regarded as a sober, industrious, and conscientious officer and not given to fantasy.

Officer Zamora was noted to be perfectly sober and somewhat agitated over his experience.

Special Agent Byrnes noted four indentations in the rough ground at the "site" of the object described by Officer Zamora. These depressions appeared regular in shape, approximately sixteen by six inches rectangular. Each depression seemed to have been made by an object going into the earth at an angle from a center line. Each depression was approximately two inches deep and pushed some earth to the far side.

Inside the four depressions were three burned patches of clumps of grass. Other clumps of grass in the same area appeared not to be disturbed. One burned area was outside the four depressions.

There were three circular marks in the earth which were smooth, approximately four inches in diameter and penetrated in the sandy earth approximately one-eighth of an inch as if a jar lid had gently been pushed into the sand.

No other person was noted in the area the night of April 24, 1964. No other objects were noted in the area possibly connected with the incident related by Officer Zamora.

So far as could be noted, there were no houses or inhabited dwellings in the area or in sight of the area.[28]

Within a few hours, the word spread, and various press reporters made their way to the site. As usually happens, many of the newspapers misconstrued the story and it quickly became a tale of aliens landing on Earth (which might not be so far-fetched after all). As the case continued to gain widespread attention and public interest, Project Blue Book director Captain Hector Quintanilla initiated a full investigation on behalf of the Air Force and directed Sergeant David Moody to go to the site and speak with Zamora. Accompanying him was Major William Connor, the officer in charge of UFO sightings and investigations at Kirkland Air Force Base. The two officers spoke with Zamora at length and it was evident from the get-go for them that this was a genuine case.

---

[28] Federal Bureau of Investigation. 1964. Review of *Unidentified Flying Object; Socorro, New Mexico; April 24, 1964*. The Black Vault. https://documents2.theblackvault.com/documents/fbifiles/paranormal/FBI-UFO-Socorro-fbi1.pdf.

Information obtained during this investigation revealed that the sighting was legitimate and there was no indication that a hoax was being perpetrated.

As part of the investigation, soil samples were collected, and data was gathered. They first checked the area for radiation, but they did not pick up any alarming radiation levels. They then collected the soil samples and sent them in for analysis, which revealed that the burned soil (from the landing site) did not contain any foreign materials or propellants. This meant that no lighter fluid or gasoline had been used to set the bush on fire. The hypothesis they considered most plausible was that the aircraft was a helicopter or military aircraft, but they communicated with several Air Force bases and they all confirmed that none of their helicopters were in the area at that time. Furthermore, no targets had been picked up on radar. The full report reads as follows:

> b. Specific Findings from Efforts to Date:
> (1) On the evening of 24 April 1964 Sgt Chavez of the New Mexico State Police accompanied by Agent Barnes of the FBI and Capt Richard Holder conducted a search of the area surrounding the sighting. There were no automobile tire markings or markings of any sort in the area other than those located at the site of the alleged landing and so noted in Capt Holder's report.
> (2) Radioactivity: Major Conner and Sgt Moody checked the area for radiation. There was no radioactivity in the area of the sighting.
> (3) Halo Activity: A check was made to determine if any helicopter activity was in the area at the approximate time of the sighting. This check was conducted at White Sands by Capt Holder who talked with the pilots and operational personnel. All helicopters at White Sands were in the hangars at the time of the sighting. Sgt Moody checked all ARS helicopters at Kirtland AFB and the landing gear did not coincide with the marks on the ground. Halo activity was checked within a radius of 300 miles including Biggs AFB at El Paso with negative results. All military halos including those associated with Project Cloud Gap have been eliminated as a possible cause of the sightings. However, civilian helicopter activity was not completely determined.

(4) <u>Radar Surveillance of the Area:</u> Capt Holder contacted radar sites at White Sands and Alamogordo. He was informed that there was no <u>unidentified</u> activity in the area during the time of the sighting.

(5) <u>Soil Samples:</u> The soil samples obtained at the sighting were given to Dr. J Allen Hynek by Capt Holder. They were turned over to Captain Quintanilla who in turn submitted them to ASD for analysis. Laboratory analysis of the soil was completed on 19 May 64. It included spectrographic analysis which revealed that there was no foreign material in the soil samples. Also, no chemicals were detected in the charred or burned soil which would indicate a type of propellant. There was no significant difference in elemental composition between the different samples.[29]

This meant that the case remained unresolved, and the aircraft and occupants Zamora had seen were still unidentified. With that being said, Captain Quintanilla was determined to solve the case. He considered another hypothesis, that the aircraft was a lunar rover or Lunar Surveyor, but this too was ruled out. At the end of the investigation they concluded that Zamora's case was unresolved, making it one of 700 cases out of the 12,618 that the Air Force investigated as part of Project Blue Book that remained unresolved. However, although the hypotheses they explored all failed to hold up, the one theory they did not consider was the extraterrestrial hypothesis. Could it be that they were unable to explain it using conventional means because it was indeed a close encounter of the third kind?

Hypotheses

Hypothesis #1: Lunar Surveyor

The first theory we shall explore is the Lunar Surveyor hypothesis. The investigations ruled out a hoax and other conventional explanations, but many skeptics have argued that the aircraft was a Lunar Surveyor being carried by a helicopter. This theory was postulated by

---

[29] Project Blue Book, National Archives—T-1206, Case 8766.

Dave Thomas, a physicist and editor at the *Skeptical Inquirer*. Before we explore this possibility, let us first examine what a Lunar Surveyor is. The Lunar Surveyor program ran between June 1966 to January 1968 and its purpose was to demonstrate and practice soft landings on Earth prior to the moon landings. The Surveyor itself has three landing pads and is equipped with several components, including a vernier engine, a solar panel, antennae, an electronic component, a television camera, an altimeter, and velocity sensing antenna. Thomas argues that what Zamora saw was in actual fact a helicopter carrying a Surveyor rover, and the two figures he saw were the pilot and engineer. He goes on to argue that the appearance of the oval aircraft could have easily been mistaken for the bulky image of the rover and helicopter. Furthermore, the bluish flames were emitted from the vernier engines while the rectangular depressions were caused by the mechanical scoop the Surveyor is equipped with.

This may seem like a rational explanation, but it does not hold true for several reasons. First, the appearance of a helicopter carrying a Surveyor is conspicuously different to the aircraft Zamora described seeing. Let us keep in mind that Zamora was in close enough proximity to the aircraft and would have been able to identify a helicopter effortlessly. Furthermore, Captain Quintanilla inquired with Air Force bases, including Wright Patterson, specifically about lunar rovers, but was still given no rational explanation. If the aircraft was indeed a Surveyor, the case would have been solved in a matter of hours. It is for this reason that Project Blue Book concluded that the case is unsolved, and the aircraft and its occupants remained unidentified.

> Initially believed to be observation of Lunar module type configuration. Effort to date cannot place vehicle at site. Case carried as UNIDENTIFIED pending additional data.[30]

Hypothesis #2: A hoax

In a letter exchange between Hynek and Dr. Donald Menzel, the possibility of the case being a prank played by students using a balloon and chemicals was discussed. Right away, it must be stated that this would

---

[30] David Thomas, "A Different Angle on the Socorro UFO of 1964", *Skeptical Inquirer*, 25(4) (2001).

have been a very elaborate and complex prank, and it is doubtful that students would have managed to pull it off. Moreover, the description of the aircraft and the figures described by Zamora do not match up with that of a balloon. Although over the years individuals have come forward claiming that they and their professor were responsible for this prank, there has been no concrete evidence to prove this. Aside from this, it is evident that this was not a balloon but an aircraft with a propulsion system. If it was just a balloon and a prank, who were the two small beings?

Hypothesis #3: The extraterrestrial hypothesis

The last hypothesis we shall explore is the extraterrestrial hypothesis: the idea that Zamora had an authentic close encounter of the third kind and the aircraft and beings were of extraterrestrial origin. First and foremost, the investigators ruled out the possibility that this case was a hoax, as well as the possibility that the aircraft was a helicopter or military aircraft. It is only because they ruled out every possibility (aside from the extraterrestrial hypothesis) that this case has remained unsolved.

The appearance of the aircraft is congruent with many UFO sightings; it is very common for individuals to describe UFOs as having an egg or an oblong shape, and this sighting is incredibly similar to Maurice Masse's encounter in Valensole, which we shall explore in the next chapter. This hypothesis is further supported by the instantaneous acceleration the aircraft performed before it disappeared. This in itself rules out the possibility of it having been a conventional aircraft. It is also possible that the two figures Zamora saw were extraterrestrials, but he did not provide a detailed description, so we cannot draw such a firm conclusion. However, Zamora did note that they had a small frame, which is a common feature described by abductees.

An imperative detail which corroborates Zamora's story and is often overlooked is the fact that there are other independent eyewitnesses, albeit coming from a secondary source. At around 18:00 on the same day as Zamora's encounter, a family of five pulled into a service station in Socorro where they spoke with Opal Grinder, the manager. As they were conversing, the man told Grinder, "Your aircraft sure fly low around here."[31] He went on to say that the aircraft "almost took the roof off our car," and he thought that the aircraft was experiencing some kind of trouble as he saw a police car drive up a hill towards its position. Two days later, as people began talking about Zamora's encounter, Grinder realized that the man at the station had described the same aircraft Zamora had seen. Many residents in the area also claimed to have heard a loud roar.

So, if the aircraft was not a military or conventional aircraft, what is the likelihood that this was indeed a close encounter of the third kind?

▲ ▼ ▲

Conclusion

Lonnie Zamora's close encounter in Socorro is indubitably one of the most compelling, credible, and pivotal cases in the study of UFOs. This is one of the 701 cases which not even the investigators at Project Blue Book could dismiss as a weather balloon or a natural phenomenon. In addition to Zamora's sincerity, credibility, and physical evidence, the case's authenticity is further validated when one considers the similarity between this account and Maurice Masse's encounter in Valensole, which took place just a year afterwards.

> There is no doubt that Lonnie Zamora saw an object which left quite an impression on him. There is also no question about Zamora's reliability. He is a serious officer, a pillar of his church, and a man well versed in recognizing airborne vehicles in his area. He is puzzled by what he saw, and frankly, so are we. This is the best documented case on record.[32]

---

[31] Jerome, Clark. *The UFO Book: Encyclopedia of the Extraterrestrial*. (Detroit, MI: Visible Ink Press, 1998), 549.
[32] Hector Quintanilla Jr., "Fall 1966: 4-37-3: The Investigation of UFOs". (College Park, MD: National Archives Identifier, 1981).

CHAPTER 5

The Valensole affair

Date: 1st July 1965
Location: Valensole, France

The vivid purple hue from the meadows of the lavender fields surrounds the commune of Valensole, making it a picturesque town in the southeast of France. In addition to the lavender fields, quaint neighborhoods, and vibrant culture, there is an extraordinary anecdote about a farmer who came into contact with otherworldly beings. This is the story of Maurice Masse, the forty-one-year-old lavender grower residing in the Provence region.

The encounter
1st of July 1965

It was the 1st of July 1965 and Masse's days started early; by dawn, he would be at his field, which was beautifully situated in the Basses Alpes, ready for a long day's work. It was around 05:30, and Masse was smoking a quick cigarette before starting his work. The idyllic silence of the early morning was harshly interrupted by a whistling noise. At that moment, Masse was standing next to a heap of rubble and he looked around to try to locate where the noise was coming from. As he turned his body, he noticed a peculiar object positioned in the middle of the field.

The object was an oval-shaped aircraft, roughly the size of a car, with a dome structure on top. Supporting it were six legs, evenly spaced around its perimeter, with a main column in its center. Many thoughts raced through Masse's mind: he had never seen such an oddly shaped aircraft before, but at the same time, it was not uncommon for military aircraft to land in his or the neighboring fields. In actual fact, he had had numerous conversations in the past with military personnel, and at first he thought that this must have been one of those instances. However, the more he looked at the object the more puzzled he became. It surely was not a helicopter since it lacked rotors, but neither could it have been an airplane due to its unconventional features … so what could it have possibly been?

A few seconds passed and he was still staring at it. He then decided to start walking towards it, when he noticed "two boys of about eight years"[33] bent over his lavender crops, picking at them. It is important to note that throughout the month of June, Masse had been finding his lavender crops with their sprouts cut off and removed from the plant, and this was extremely infuriating for him. He finally thought that he had caught the culprits, so he started walking ardently towards them, ready to confront them. When he was about six meters away from them, the two figures straightened up and one of them pointed a cylindrical instrument at him, paralyzing him on the spot. He could not move a muscle—he had completely lost control over his body.

As he stared ahead, he took in all of their obscure features and he quickly realized that these beings were not children and were certainly not human beings either. Despite having the stature and size similar to that of an eight-year-old child, they had massive, bald "pumpkin-like heads."[34] Their large, slanted eyes contrasted with their small mouths and pointed chins. Masse was immobilized, with every passing second feeling like an hour, and all he could do was just look ahead at them.

---

[33] Ralph Blum and Judy Blum, *Beyond Earth: Man's Contact with UFOs*. (New York: Bantam Books, 1974), 179.

[34] Aimé Michel and Charles Bowen, "A Visit to Valensole", *Flying Saucer Review*, 14(1) (1968).

He noticed how the two beings appeared to be communicating with each other using grunt-like noises coming from their abdomen. After a few moments, the two beings dashed inside the aircraft, which quickly started ascending from the ground and then shot up toward the sky, disappearing in an instant.

For the next fifteen minutes, Masse was left dumbfounded, unaware of what the next course of action should be. This was a bizarre and unprecedented experience and he was certain no one would believe his story. Nor did he have any intention of telling anyone either. He looked around the field and noticed that the aircraft had left discernable depressions and landing marks on the ground. At the very least, this proved that what he had witnessed had actually happened. After regaining his composure, Masse made his way to the village, to the Café des Sports, a local establishment owned by a friend, who immediately noticed that something was off with Masse as he looked agitated and on edge. Although he was very hesitant about it, Masse told his friend what he had just experienced; he described the oval-shaped aircraft and its landing, but he omitted the interaction he had had with the two beings.

Everyone in the village knew Masse to be a sincere and genuine individual, and his friend was certain that he would not have made up such a tale. The only suggestion he could offer was to report it to the gendarmerie, but Masse immediately dismissed the suggestion; he knew full well that if he were to talk about it, people around the village would soon learn about the story and this was the last thing Masse wanted. Masse tried downplaying the story as a joke, but his anxiety and agitation showed that he was being truthful. Within a few hours, word started spreading among the villagers and Masse's encounter quickly became the topic of discussion. Later that evening, at around 20:30, Masse returned to the field with his daughter; there he noticed that the soil in the depressions had hardened like cement.

The investigation

The following day, Masse's encounter was a hot topic among the villagers. Even the local gendarmerie had heard of his story and contacted Masse to inquire further. Below is an excerpt from Masse's witness statement.

A moment later, I heard a whistle not far from me. At that time, I was hiding behind a pile of stones. I saw absolutely nothing after the whistle; I headed where it seemed to come from, and I then noticed that the machine was placed in my lavender field. it was the size of a [Renault] Dauphine car, and dull in color. Its shape resembled a rugby ball with a zippered door on the side. The top was made of transparent material through which I saw a person inside.

When I saw the aircraft, a man was already on the ground. He was dressed in a jumpsuit it seems, his head bare, his hands empty. I was about sixty meters away. The height of this character was about one meter. The passenger of the machine probably noticed me because I suppose he warned the one who was on the ground, who immediately got back into the machine. It then made a dull noise and the machine disappeared almost immediately in the direction of Manosque.

I continued to work, then approaching the location where the aircraft had landed, I noticed that the ground was soaked. Traces having the shape of a star were apparent. A hole about 80 centimeters deep and 40 centimeters in diameter was in the center of the site. When stopped, it seemed to me that the device was placed on six legs placed below and a steel-colored peg in the center. No porthole; only a sliding door opening from top to bottom.

I specify that when the person who was on the ground got into the device, he put his right hand forward to grab hold of the edge of the opening of the device. The machine left obliquely; I lost sight of him after ten to fifteen meters. It was about six to eight meters high when I no longer saw it. I looked up to see where he might have been, but I couldn't see him anymore. He disappeared worse than a flash. When it took off, the six legs which rested on the ground and which made the device look like a spider, gave me the impression of spinning all in the same sound ...[35]

The officials asked to visit the lavender field, and he did not object. At the site they observed the landing marks: there was a cylindrical hole in the center which was forty centimeters deep and eighteen centimeters wide. Although Masse described the aircraft as having six legs, only

[35] Region Gendarm Marseille. 1965. Review of *Synthese Journalière—Situation En 9 Rm le 3/7/65.* GEIPAN.fr. https://geipan.fr/sites/default/files/PV%20n%C2%B0445%20 %281965309761%29.pdf.

four markings were located, each around eight centimeters wide, forming the shape of a cross with the cylindrical hole in the center.

> 41-year-old farmer declares having seen a Dauphine-size "Flying
> Saucer" type machine with two passengers—Individual, height
> approximately 1m, strong build, dressed in overalls, bareheaded,
> would have descended from the machine for a few moments—
> Then the machine would have disappeared suddenly at lightning
> speed—Declaration made at Gendarmerie on 2.7.65 at 8 p.m.—On
> the spot, Captain observed traces that could possibly correspond to
> the actual laying of the machine.[36]

On the fourth day after the encounter, things took a troubling turn.
Masse started experiencing intense physiological ailments; whereas he
usually got four to five hours of sleep at night, he now slept for hours
on end. He felt lethargic and experienced throbbing headaches, and
at one point he even collapsed. Masse also developed psychomotor
impairment, and these symptoms were observed and noted by the gen-
darmeric too. After giving his witness statement to the officials, Masse
presumed that things would resume to normal and he would return
back to his quiet life, but as he would find out, it was not so easy to put
this bizarre experience behind him.

As the days passed, people continued to talk about it and Masse
remained in the spotlight. He was unaccustomed to this and felt uneasy
about this newfound attention, so he decided to go to Giens with his
wife for a few days to escape the press, but even there he was followed
by reporters who questioned him endlessly about his experience. Masse
realized at that point that the only way he would be left alone and able
to move on was if he gave the reporters what they wanted: the full story.

The full story

It was the 8th of August, around a month after his encounter when
Masse met with a renowned UFO researcher in France, Aimé Michel.
During this meeting, Masse recounted his story in its entirety, includ-
ing the close encounter with the two humanoid beings. He described

---

[36] Ibid.

their grotesque characteristics and how they had rendered him immobile. Although this encounter was frightening, Masse explained how he was certain that they had good intentions and that at no point did he fear for his safety. Interestingly, during this interview, Michel noted that Masse's watch had a three-degree deviation when he put a compass over it. Despite the fact that this deviation is common for steel watches, it is certainly intriguing, and I wonder if it existed prior to the encounter or if it could have been caused by the aircraft's propulsion system. One of the biggest pieces of evidence supporting the idea that an unconventional aircraft had landed in Masse's field was the implied change in the soil structure. In contrast to the purple hue of the lavender crops, within the landing site, only withered weeds continued to grow.

> They are good. They have only good intentions towards us, of that
> I am sure. I don't know how I know. But I am sure of it.[37]

Masse's encounter remained a fascinating story among UFO enthusiasts and a peculiar tale among the locals. Two years after the encounter, Aimé Michel returned to Valensole for a follow-up interview with Masse. Accompanying him this time was Charles Bowen from the *Flying Saucer Review*. During this second meeting, Michel made a noteworthy observation: whereas two years prior Masse seemed perturbed and agitated when recounting his story, he now seemed calm and at ease. As part of the interview, Michel and Bowen visited "l'Olivol," Masse's lavender field. Two years had now passed and there was still evidence that something strange had occurred in the field as only weeds continued to grow around the landing site.

In the previous chapter we analyzed Lonnie Zamora's close encounter in Socorro, New Mexico, and one can see several similarities between the two cases, including the oval-shaped aircraft, the description of the two occupants and their behavior. Michel was aware of this similarity and thus he showed Masse the sketch Zamora had drawn of the aircraft, and upon seeing it, Masse was taken aback and was in total disbelief. He was convinced that Zamora had seen the same aircraft he had. This discovery was imperative for Masse; although there was the physical evidence to corroborate his story, the fact that another individual from another continent had experienced such a similar encounter proved above everything else that this phenomenon occurred on a global scale.

---

[37] Aimé Michel, "The Valensole Affair", *Flying Saucer Review*, 11(6) (1965).

Masse was at his last gasp, as though he had just looked upon his own death. At first, he thought that somebody had photographed his machine. When he learnt that this one had been seen in the United States by a policeman, he seemed relieved and said to me: "You see then that I wasn't dreaming and that I am not mad."[38]

Although this was the first time Masse had described his close encounter in great detail, Michel still felt a sense of hesitancy from Masse's end and believed that he was withholding some details. This was indeed the case, and Masse told him numerous times that there are certain aspects of his experience which he would not tell anyone, not even his wife.

What I have not told you, I have not told anybody, not even my wife, and nobody will make me tell. Do not insist on it and let us say no more about it.[39]

Over a decade later, in May of 1979, renowned author and researcher Jacques Vallée spoke with Masse. In the interview, Masse recounted his experience and stated that he had seen the aircraft on other occasions, but not the occupants. Even ten years later, Masse meticulously answered questions and refused to divulge all the details of his encounter. To this day, Masse's full story has remained untold.

... it is clear that Masse has never told the entire truth about his experience ...[40]

Hypotheses

Hypothesis #1: A misidentification?

Could it be that the aircraft Masse reported seeing was in actual fact a military helicopter? Many skeptics have suggested this as a possibility, but this hypothesis is preposterous for several reasons. To begin with, the description of the aircraft Masse saw does not match up with that of

---

[38] Michel and Bowen, "A Visit to Valensole", *Flying Saucer Review*, 14(1) (1968).
[39] Ibid.
[40] Jacques Vallée, *Confrontations: A Scientist's Search for Alien Contact*. (New York: Ballantine Books, 1990).

a helicopter as it lacked rotors and a visible propulsion system. It also performed a rapid vertical ascent and disappeared in an instant, which naturally is a maneuver a helicopter cannot perform. Furthermore, who or what were the two beings? This hypothesis also does not account for the immediate and intermediate aftereffects reported by Masse, including the drastic change in his behavior, the landing marks at the field as well as the implied change in the soil's structure.

Hypothesis #2: A hoax?

It is impossible to conclusively determine the authenticity of a close encounter or other events which are regarded as "paranormal" (the word "paranormal" refers to events or phenomena which fall outside the realm of what can be scientifically explained). We must thus explore whether Masse could have fabricated the story. This is naturally a possibility, but it does not make sense in this circumstance for several reasons. Masse avoided public attention as much as he possibly could, and he only discussed his story as he believed it would stop the media from hounding him for answers. Even then, Masse did not divulge all of the details. Thus, what would have been the purpose of this hoax? Masse did not gain fame or money from it.

Hypothesis #3: The extraterrestrial hypothesis

The extraterrestrial hypothesis is supported by several factors, including the description of the aircraft and its occupants, the landing marks, the change in soil structure, the immediate and intermediate aftereffects, and lastly, Masse's sincerity. Immediately after the encounter, Masse observed a deep cylindrical hole in the center of the landing site and four shallow depressions surrounding it. This observation was noted by the gendarmes too. In addition to this, the crops in the area around the landing site had all withered, and this anomaly persisted for years after the encounter. This discovery establishes a direct correlation between the aircraft's propulsion system and the change in soil structure. Moreover, Masse began to experience intense lethargy four days after the encounter; whereas he used to sleep four to five hours per day, he now slept for several more hours on end. A few days after the event, he even began to experience psychomotor agitation, despite the fact that tests revealed that this was not the result of a neuro-degenerative disease.

The biggest factor which corroborates the extraterrestrial hypothesis is the presence and description of the humanoid beings Masse reported seeing. The description of these beings is akin to the stereotypical features of extraterrestrial beings, as we shall continue to see throughout this book. It is imperative to note that Masse never intended for his story to reach the press. As a matter of fact, his encounter is one of the lesser known, and this is because he never sought fame or money.

▲ ▼ ▲

Conclusion

Masse's sincerity and honesty are unequivocal, and when combined with the physical evidence, this case ranks among the most credible close encounters of the third kind. It is cases like this one, where Masse withheld from disclosing the full story to the public, that make me wonder about the implications of the phenomenon, especially when it comes to human consciousness and spirituality. What was so astounding or personal that Masse refused to divulge and share it with the world? It is without a doubt a shame that we will never find out; however, Masse's extraordinary encounter in the lavender fields undoubtedly had a transformative effect on him.

CHAPTER 6

The Ariel school landing

Date: 16th September 1994
Location: Ruwa, Zimbabwe

The month of September, 1994, was an unusual period in Zimbabwe, with many people reporting seeing bright fireballs and unidentified lights in the sky. In fact, the southern part of Africa was inundated with UFO reports throughout the month. In the weeks that followed, radio stations received phone calls from hundreds of people claiming to have seen these fireballs, and while they were dismissed as meteorites, nothing could discredit the report that came on the 16th of September. What follows is the extraordinary encounter of sixty-two schoolchildren who claimed to have seen an extraterrestrial aircraft and its occupants land adjacent to their school yard. Is this a true otherworldly encounter, or merely a story that has evolved over time?

The UFO flap
14th September 1994

Wednesday, 14th September 1994 was an exciting night for southern Africa. Round about 20:50 to 21:05 hours, a pyrotechnic display
of some magnificence appeared in the almost clear night skies of
this part of the continent.[41]

Throughout the month of September, many people in Zimbabwe and
the southern part of Africa reported seeing strange lights in the sky,
including balls of fire and white and goldish lights traveling in formation then abruptly changing direction. At the time, this wave of UFO
reports appeared to have peaked on Wednesday, 14th September.
On the day, at around 20:50, many people saw three large lights with
smaller lights trailing them, moving from the north to the south. However, to the dismay of many UFO researchers, there was a very prosaic
explanation for these sightings; on the same day, the Zenit-2 rocket from
the Cosmos 2290 satellite ejected its cone, and this is most likely what
many people had seen in the sky. However, there was still a significant
number of reports which did not quite fit this description.

Unbeknown to everyone, this was only just the beginning of what
proved to be an eventful few months in Zimbabwe; just two days later,
more than sixty children would report seeing an unidentified aircraft
and its occupants outside their school yard, making this one of the most
peculiar and captivating close encounters in history.

▲ ▼ ▲

The encounter

My impression is that the children, and I spoke to many of the 62
witnesses, were telling the truth, although there might have been
some embroidery from the more imaginative ones; but on the
whole, their evidence was straight forward and convincing.[42]

---

[41] Cynthia Hind, "UFO Flap in Zimbabwe," UFO AFRINEWS, 11 (February 1995).
[42] Cynthia Hind, "Recent UFO Sightings in Africa—The Cultural Implications," UFOs:
Examining the Evidence: The Proceedings of 8th BUFORA International UFO Congress, 1995,
https://bufora.org.uk/documents/1995UFOsExaminingtheevidence.8thInternational
conference.pdf.

To fully understand this encounter and the events that transpired, I will be presenting the details and timeline of events in a chronological order. The incident took place at an elementary school named Ariel, located in Ruwa, Zimbabwe. An imperative detail which must be emphasized is the fact that even after all these years, no one involved in the encounter has come forward to claim that the event was a hoax or that they were not telling the truth. Their testimonies have remained unchanged since the day of the encounter.

Friday, 16th September 1994

The incident took place on Friday the 16th of September 1994. The day was seemingly as ordinary as any other, and while the teachers held their staff meeting inside, the students were having their recess outside in the school yard. The time was around 10:15, and at one moment, a number of children started looking up at the sky as they saw a bright light. This bright light turned out to be a large, circular aircraft surrounded by several smaller ones. According to the children's reports, there were as many as three silver objects surrounding the larger circular one.

The circular aircraft were hovering just outside the school yard above the adjacent field, and as they continued to hover, some children became apprehensive and ran inside, while others moved closer with curiosity. The incident did not end there, and it is the details that follow that make this encounter so compelling. As the aircraft landed, many children reported seeing two beings standing outside the aircraft (some of the children claimed one of the beings was on top of the aircraft, while others claimed it was on the ground). The children's descriptions of the beings varied, as did their drawings of them, but they were generally described as being around five foot six inches tall, with pale, translucent skin. The children further stated that they had long, black hair and protruding, black, almond-shaped eyes. The two creatures were dressed in a black, tight-fitted suit, similar to that of a diver. The beings and the aircraft vanished as swiftly as they had appeared. The encounter lasted about fifteen minutes and in total sixty-two children stated that they had seen the aircraft in the sky (the number of children who reported seeing the beings, however, is lower than that).

As the beings and aircraft disappeared, many of the children were petrified by what they had witnessed and ran inside the school to inform their teachers. Many of the teachers were initially skeptical of the story and tried to reassure the children. However, as more children came forward with the same exact story, the teachers realized it was highly unlikely that all of these children had concocted the same exact story with such specificity. Furthermore, while their descriptions differed slightly, they all described the same encounter from their subjective point of view. As the school day came to an end, the parents began to hear about what had happened and word quickly spread. While some parents dismissed the story, believing it was simply their child's imagination, others inquired with the teachers. This added even more intrigue around the recent UFO flap, and the story even reached the BBC. A few hours later, Tim Leach, a correspondent of the BBC in Zimbabwe heard the story. He was unsure how to approach such a piece, so he contacted Cynthia Hind, a well-known UFO researcher and MUFON's field investigator and coordinator for the entire continent of Africa.

Saturday, 17th September 1994

The following day, Cynthia spoke with the first eyewitness, Alyson Kirkman, who was working at the tuckshop at the time. Alyson told Cynthia how one of the twelve-year-old children ran into the shop and told her that he had seen "a man in a silver suit with a band around his head, running around the playground."[43] Alyson, not knowing what to make of the story was skeptical at first, but then other children told her the same exact story, including her daughter.

Ten-year-old Fifi Kirkman was outside in the school yard at the time of the incident, and she later told her mother how she had seen a silvery-white light hovering behind the trees in the field adjacent to their yard. The light was emitting a whirring noise and after a few moments it landed on the ground. Although Fifi did not see the creatures herself, many of her friends did. After speaking with Alyson and Fifi, Cynthia phoned the school headmaster, Colin Mackie, and asked him to have the children draw what they had seen first thing on Monday morning. They also arranged for Cynthia and her assistant, Gunter Hofer, to visit the school on Tuesday to meet and speak with some of the students and to also inspect the landing site.

---

[43] Ibid.

Monday, 19th September 1994

Colin Mackie gathered the children in a classroom first thing on Monday morning, just as Cynthia had suggested, and asked them to draw what they had seen the previous Friday. More than sixty drawings were made, and they are compelling to say the least. Interestingly, they are also relatively consistent; many of the drawings feature a large circular object in the foreground with two or three smaller, circular aircraft in the sky. The aircraft on the ground is depicted as having an oval shape with portholes around its circumference. Some of the drawings also include the creature that many of the children claimed to have seen. The creature depicted in the drawings resembles a typical extraterrestrial being, with a disproportionately large head and dark, slanted eyes. In some of the drawings the being has long, black hair.

Later on the same day, Tim Leach from the BBC and his crew visited the school where he spoke with three of the children, Guy, Kayleigh, and Oriana as well as the headmaster, Colin Mackie. The following is the complete transcript of Leach's interview with the children. This is also the first interview regarding the incident.

Leach	Could you tell me what you saw on Friday?
Kayleigh	Well we saw some people. There was a white one, a weird one, and a black one and the black one was sitting on the spaceship.
Leach	How did you know it was a spaceship? It wasn't a helicopter or something like that?
Guy	Well, it looked like it was glinting in the trees. It looked roundabout like a like a disc, like a roundabout like a disk. Like a round.
Leach	And whereabouts was it?
Guy	It was in the trees over there, between the third pole.
Leach	And you say it looked like a disk. Are you sure it wasn't a Harrier jump jet, or an aircraft, something the Zimbabwe Air Force have got?
Guy	No, it was like in a disk.
Leach	And what happened, Guy?
Guy	Well, it was just glinting in the trees and there was a man, and he walked toward us, and he walked back again.
Leach	What did he look like?

Guy   His face was like this (makes an oval shape) and his eyes were down here (touches the cheeks).

Leach   What, further down his face?

Guy   Yeah, much further down than us because our eyes are here, his were down.

Leach   And how close were you to him?

Guy   Well, I was like at the back because I just been finished in the classroom and I was quite at the back. So, all the other kids were in the front.

Leach   You don't think it was somebody in fancy dress doing a prank or something?

Guy   No.

Leach   What about you Oriana? Tell us what you saw.

Oriana I saw the same as Guy but under the silver glittery thing I saw this black—looks like a stick but was very thin.

Leach   It was a man was it?

Oriana I don't know what it was but it was very thin. All I saw was like a long thing on a like silver thing.

Guy   And he was very very thin.

Leach   Do you think he was a black Zimbabwean man?

Guy   No, not really. He wasn't very very dark, he was very—quite lightish and he was very thin.

Leach   How tall about?

Guy   About, say, there (holds up hand up above his head).

Leach   Just a bit taller than you?

Guy   Well yeah.

Leach   Why do you think that this was something different, this wasn't some helicopter from the Zimbabwe Air Force, and just some guys playing a joke—why do you think it was actually a UFO and possibly a spaceman?

Guy   It was just because it was—somebody wouldn't just be playing around and just be on the ground all of a sudden.

Leach   Did it make any noise, this thing?

Guy   Not really, no.

Leach   And it landed? Something landed? Did you see it land?

Guy   No, it was in the trees over there, like in the trees like glinting. And like there was somebody on the ground.

Leach   And then what happened?

Guy	And then he walked towards us and he walked back again and they just went.
Leach	How? How did they go?
Guy	It just went all of a sudden.
Leach	What, like a helicopter?
Guy	No, just went.
Leach	Which way?
Guy	Down—more down into the valley.
Leach	At about what height?
Guy	Quite high.
Leach	And then what happened?
Guy	And then it didn't come back again.
Leach	And did you girls see that as well?
Girls	Yes.
Leach	So, you're the headmaster of Ariel school, tell me, what do you think of all of this?
Mackie	I feel sure that the children feel that they did see something. I don't believe or disbelieve to be completely honest, but I do feel that they definitely saw something. We had a number of children say they did, we asked them to draw pictures of what they saw this morning, what they saw on Friday, and after looking at them, I definitely feel that they did see something. I agree that it could be something that we are not common with, but to actually say it was a UFO, I would be reluctant to say something like that. I personally did not see it.[44]

The above transcript is essential for understanding the development of the story. Thus far, two questions arise: did the aircraft land on the ground or did it remain hovering in the sky? Second, did it emit a noise or not? An important detail in this interview is Kayleigh's comments regarding the creatures; she stated that she saw a total of three beings, "a white one, a weird one, and a black one". Many of the children reported seeing two creatures in total, both dressed in a tight-fitted black suit. The creatures' skin was described as pale, almost translucent-like,

---

[44] Charlie Wiser, "Ariel School—First on the Scene," Three-Dollar Kit, 2022, https://three-dollarkit.weebly.com/ariel-first-on-the-scene.html.

so it could be the case that this is what Kayleigh was referring to with the "white one" and "black one."

Tuesday, 20th September 1994

On Tuesday, Cynthia Hind, her assistant Gunter Hofer, and Tim Leach visited Ariel and the alleged landing site. Cynthia also spoke with the grade sevens, the eldest group of children who witnessed the encounter. Nathaniel, the first eyewitness, reported seeing "a ship, landed on the ground"; he described the ship as having a long top with a "platform" around the side. Nathaniel also mentioned seeing a "black man running around" who appeared to be their size. Luke also reported seeing the creature. Although he did not see the aircraft himself, he told Cynthia that the "little black guy" was wearing all black and "looked like he had long hair." Daniel witnessed the aircraft and creature as well; he described the being as being "fairly plump." He, too, made a remark about its hair, comparing it to that of a "hippie."

Emily's account of what happened is interesting. "I saw the little black men," Emily said to Cynthia. She went on to say that "they had longish hair and it was all black. And they had big black eyes. That's all I saw. I saw a glimpse. They kind of turned around and stared and then went back into a kind of like ship. There was like sort of one big one and quite a few little ones scattered alone." Emily also described the feeling of terror she experienced. When Cynthia asked Emily what she thought the beings were, Emily stated that everyone was saying they were UFOs and admitted that this had influenced her belief. Having said that, she did reiterate that she definitely did see the aircraft and the beings. Charity, another grade seven student, described seeing the silver, saucer-shaped aircraft. Charity stated that she had never heard of UFOs prior to the incident and that this was a completely new topic to her.

Emma's account is incredibly detailed, as is her drawing. She described seeing several objects in the sky that hovered a meter above the ground before disappearing. She also described seeing a "shiny black" creature who wore a tight-fitted suit. The most discernible feature was its large eyes. When asked what she thought the creature was, Emma stated that she "thought it was some kind of alien from a different planet." During the conversation with the children and teachers, it was also revealed that the children had also seen a UFO the day before the incident, on Thursday. Mr. Mackie told Cynthia how many of the children had told him that they had seen the unconventional aircraft on Thursday as well, but some of them were too shy to speak up about it.

I must also acknowledge Cynthia's choice of words when speaking with the children as it does seem that she asked leading questions and was prompting the children to give the answers she wanted to hear. I am not claiming that the children were coerced into saying that the aircraft and beings were extraterrestrial, but it appears that this response was encouraged. For instance, Cynthia told the children that this is "the biggest story of the twentieth century" and that "America had gotten in touch with her." Although this is truly an extraordinary story and case, hyping it up that way in front of the children could have caused them to dramatize the details. She did acknowledge the Russian satellite and how it could have been the aircraft they had seen, but she went on to tell them that this "would not account for the figure you saw" and that "it is time the world woke up, that something's going on and they don't all think I'm a kooky character." Having said that, it should be noted that this interview took place on Tuesday, whereas the children had been providing the same, exact narrative since Friday.

As part of the visit, Cynthia and her assistant Gunter also visited the landing site with a makeshift Geiger counter. The resources in Zimbabwe were limited and they did not have access to an actual Geiger counter; so, Gunter created his own instrument that detected radiation levels. As they went to the field adjacent to the school ground where the aircraft had allegedly landed, they were unable to detect any landing marks or unusual radiation readings.[45]

Friday and Saturday, 2nd and 3rd December 1994

Cynthia Hind was correct in saying that this story amassed a lot of attention and excitement—in reality, a story cannot get any bigger than sixty-two children claiming to have seen a UFO and its alien occupants. John Mack, a renowned psychiatrist and the head of Harvard's department of psychiatry, heard about the encounter and became intrigued; he flew to Zimbabwe on the next available flight to speak with the children himself. Although over two months had passed, the children's memory

---

[45] *Ariel School UFO Landing 1994, YouTube,* 2012, https://youtube.com/watch?v= eBqKJHSrYZg.

of what happened on the 14th September remained vivid in their heads. Their story remained unchanged, but a new detail emerged: Mack was told by many of the children that the being communicated with them telepathically and warned them about pollution and its harmful effects on the environment. Hailey, one of the eyewitnesses, told Mack that she was "very scared" that the "aliens would attack [her]." Hailey was not the only eyewitness who felt this fear; in fact, this was a common emotion felt by the majority of the children. As we can see from the following dialogue, Emma had similar feelings, and she also revealed to Mack how the being had communicated with her telepathically:

Emma No. My heart kind of went faster and then slower and then faster and then slower all at the same time.

Mack Now was that excitement?

Emma Yeah, excitement and scariness.

Mack And scary. And you said happy too?

Emma Yeah.

Mack Happy because?

Emma Because I saw something strange and something peculiar and something nobody had ever seen. The other man, his eyes looked at me as if uh, "I want you." And things like that.

Mack I want to what?

Emma I want you.

Mack I want you. I want you in what? Like I want you to come with me? Or?

Emma Yeah. I want you to come with me. I want you to come.

Mack Did you go with him, do you think?

Emma No, only my eyes went with him.

Mack Your eyes went with him.

Emma And my feeling.

Mack And your feeling went with him. So, was there a part of you that wanted to go with him?

Emma Yeah.

Mack That felt like drawn to go with him?

Emma Yeah.

Mack Okay, can you say what that felt like?

Emma Again, scary and a little excited, and a little I shouldn't go.

Mack Yeah.

Emma He was just staring and we like tried not to look at him, 'cause he was quite scary.

Mack   What was scary about him?

Emma   His big eyes, I think. I think they want um people to know that we're actually making harm on this world and we mustn't get too technolodged?

Mack   What gave you that feeling?

Emma   I don't know.

Mack   But it came through to you when you were with the strange being?

Emma   Yeah. When he was looking at me,

Mack   When he was looking at you.

Emma   Yeah.

Mack   How did that get communicated to you?

Emma   I don't know.

Mack   But somehow it did.

Emma   Yeah, it came through my head.

Mack   Through your head. Like through words or?

Emma   My conscience, I think.

Mack   Your what?

Emma   My conscience told me.

Mack   Your conscience told you?

Emma   Yeah.

Mack   While you were …

Emma   While I was …

Mack   … in contact with the being, do you mean, or when?

Emma   While the being was looking at me.

Mack   While it was looking at you, your conscience told you that. Had you been a person that thought a lot about what we're doing to the Earth before that?

Emma   No. Only after this.

Lisel, another student who saw the being, stated that looking into his black eyes made her "think the world was going to end," and that the being was warning them of what was to come … it felt like a premonition of some sort. As a follow up to this, Mack asked her if these beings wanted us to be scared, to which Lisel replied, "Maybe, because we don't look after the planet, the air properly." Lisel, like Emma, told Mack how she had never thought about this topic before and that this fear and contemplation only began after the being communicated these messages to her. Lisel went on to say that she felt terrible and that "all the trees will just go down, and there will be no air, and people will be dying." Francis reiterated the same message—he told Mack how these beings came to Earth because something involving "pollution" was about to happen.[46]

After John Mack's visit to Ariel school, the encounter and incident became a cornerstone in UFO research. The Ariel school sighting is now widely considered as one of the most compelling and convincing cases of a close encounter ever documented. More than fifty children reported the same story, which has remained consistent over the years to this very day. Before delving into the possible hypotheses, I will first go over some observations, facts about the incident, and also address common questions that have been raised by many over the years. This will help us to have a complete picture of the facts and of the story.

▲ ▼ ▲

How many eyewitnesses were there?

Cynthia Hind reported that sixty-two children witnessed the aircraft on Friday. However, the number of children who claimed to have seen the beings is lower than that.

How many UFO sightings were there?

On Wednesday the 14th of September, many people over Zimbabwe and the southern part of Africa reported seeing strange lights in the sky, although this could have been the Zenit-2 rocket, as has been mentioned. During Cynthia's visit to Ariel on Tuesday the 20th of September, headmaster Colin Mackie stated that in addition to the aircraft the children reportedly saw on Friday, he had also been told by many students that they had seen another unconventional aircraft the day before.

How many UFOs did the children see?

The children's accounts differ, but they all mention seeing more than one aircraft. The majority of testimonies describe one large aircraft surrounded by smaller ones.

---

[46] Charlie Wiser, "Dr John Mack Interviews," Three-Dollar Kit, 2022, https://threedollarkit.weebly.com/ariel-mack.html.

How many beings were there and what did they look like?

Again, the children's accounts differ, but the vast majority reported seeing two beings, both of which had pale, translucent skin, protruding, black, almond-shaped eyes, long black hair, and were dressed in a black tight-fitted suit.

How long did the encounter last?

Colin Mackie stated that the encounter lasted fifteen minutes.

Were the children aware of UFOs?

Yes, some of the standard fours even had a class discussion on UFOs earlier that week. Could this have influenced their narrative? Certainly; however, this does not imply that the children fabricated the entire story either.

▲ ▼ ▲

Hypotheses

There have been numerous theories and hypotheses proposed in relation to the Ariel school sighting. Many people believe that this is a genuine close encounter of the third kind while skeptics believe that this is nothing more than the product of the children's imagination. In this section of the chapter, we will carefully examine each hypothesis and the supporting evidence for each theory.

Hypothesis #1: An imaginative story

The first hypothesis we shall explore suggests that this encounter is nothing more than a story that has evolved and became more detailed and imaginative over time. Could it be that the children first saw a UFO and then embellished their story to gain more traction? Children do have an imaginative mind, so what if this is all just an inventive story that has evolved over time?

A big factor which supports this theory is the sheer lack of evidence. There were no landing marks, no abnormal radiation levels or any other indications that an unconventional aircraft had landed in the adjacent field. This, however, does not outright invalidate the corroborated narrative of sixty-two children. The second factor which supports this theory is the fact that the children were primed to believe that the aircraft and beings were extraterrestrial in origin, and I will explain how. Throughout the week of the encounter there was a surge in UFO sightings across Zimbabwe and some of the children even had a class discussion on the topic. Could it be that some of the kids simply saw a shiny object in the sky and assumed it was an extraterrestrial aircraft? Could it be that one of the children claimed to have seen a being, leading many others to believe that they had as well? Many believe that as the story gained more attention and people like Cynthia Hind spoke with the children, the children were encouraged to believe and claim that they had encountered an extraterrestrial entity.

This hypothesis appears to be logical, but it is debatable for a number of reasons. I want to again acknowledge that Cynthia Hind did indeed ask leading questions and some of her comments could be interpreted as though she was encouraging the children to believe in the extraterrestrial hypothesis. However, Cynthia spoke with the children on Tuesday, and the children mentioned the aircraft and the strange beings immediately after the encounter on Friday. During the interview with Tim Leach on Monday, Kayleigh made reference to a "spaceship" and Guy, Oriana, and Kayleigh each made reference to the being dressed in black. So, it is simply incorrect to claim that Cynthia anchored the extraterrestrial story into the minds of these children in order to influence their narrative. The only detail that changed over time in the children's narrative, from the day of the landing to several decades later, was the communication with the being. The children initially made no mention of one of the beings communicating with them telepathically. This detail was only revealed when psychiatrist John Mack paid a visit in December. But does the fact that they only revealed this detail months later imply that they made it up? It should also be noted that it was not just one child who made this comment, but several children stated that the being communicated with them telepathically. Furthermore, to this day, not a single witness has come forward and claimed that this was a hoax.

Hypothesis #2: A prank

Could it be that the children were telling the truth but were mistaken in thinking that the aircraft and beings were extraterrestrial in origin? What if the beings were just other children playing a prank, or even a puppet show, as some have suggested? Although this could have been the case, thus far no one has come forward to claim they were responsible for this prank.

Hypothesis #3: The extraterrestrial hypothesis

What if the children were telling the truth and they were right in believing that the aircraft and beings originated from another planet? What if the UFO flap is a corroborating piece of evidence? There is a probability that this is indeed the case, and many people point to one single factor to support this claim: it is extremely unlikely that sixty-two children would tell the same, corroborated story and that none of them would come forward decades later to claim that it was a hoax. It is important to note that no one, not even the teachers, has claimed that this incident was a hoax or a publicity stunt.

Furthermore, another factor which proves that the children were being truthful in their narrative is their descriptions. Many will point out that their narratives and descriptions differed slightly, which is correct; however, this only proves that they were being truthful. If all of the children had recounted the same, exact detail, it would have indicated that they had agreed on what to mention beforehand, but this was not the case; the details varied because each child naturally experienced the encounter from a different point of view. Lastly, we must also acknowledge the telepathic message which the being communicated with the children, that pollution will eradicate the planet. This is a common experience among abductees, and we will come across this theme in subsequent chapters as well.

Conclusion

The Ariel school sighting is a fascinating case shrouded in mystery and intrigue, but, as with many of the cases discussed in this book, there is no conclusive evidence to determine whether or not this was a genuine close encounter. In actual fact, there are many questions which have been left unanswered. Did the children truly see an extraterrestrial aircraft and its occupants? If this was all a hoax, then how come no one has come forward all these decades later? In 1994, sixty-two children provided a narrative which has remained consistent ever since.

Thirty years later, these adults spoke about the encounter and their narrative has stayed consistent. The aircraft, the beings, the telepathic messages—all of these details have remained unchanged.

At the end of this chapter, after all of the details and potential hypotheses have been presented, what do you make of this encounter? Do you believe these sixty-two children and their story? Is it possible for so many children to conjure up such a credible story and keep it up for decades? It is these questions which make the Ariel school sighting such a pivotal case in the study of close encounters.

PART 2

ALIEN ABDUCTIONS

CHAPTER 7

Introduction

The cases I chose for this section are widely regarded as the most compelling and significant alien abduction cases in history. Before delving into the cases, we will first examine the sequence of a typical alien abduction. As I stated in the beginning of this book, if genuine UFO sightings are rare, genuine alien abduction cases are even more so. A very valid question many people ask is: how do you determine whether an alien abduction story is real or not? As I carried out the research for this book, I analyzed a number of cases (those included in this book as well as several others that were not), and after thoroughly investigating this phenomenon, I devised a list of factors that determine whether a case is authentic or not.

The stages of an alien abduction

Stage 1: UAP sighting

The alien abduction typically starts off with a general UFO sighting; the individual will describe seeing strange lights or unconventional aircraft in the sky. Many of the five observables aforementioned in this book are typically present, which indicate that the aircraft is of extraterrestrial origin rather than a misidentification or terrestrial aircraft.

Stage 2: Immobilization

The individual will then notice that the UFO is gradually approaching their position, and as it inches closer, they will be able to make out its unconventional and peculiar characteristics more clearly. Furthermore, many abductees have reported feeling immobilized where they feel a sense of complete powerlessness over their body, as if some force has taken control over them. They are consumed by fear and terror, and despite their mind telling them to flee the scene, they are unable to do so; all they can do is stare ahead and watch what is happening right in front of their eyes.

Stage 3: The aliens

As the person becomes immobile, a sinister creature (or creatures) with bizarre and grotesque features appears. From the get-go, due to the overt features, the individual is able to discern that this being is of extraterrestrial origin. The entities are commonly described as looking humanoid, standing around five foot tall with disproportionately large heads, bulging, almond-shaped, dark eyes, and a small slit for a mouth. Surprisingly, despite their terrifying appearance, many abductees have reportedly received reassuring telepathic messages assuring them that they will not be harmed and will be returned safely.

Stage 4: The capture

The individual is then captured and escorted onto the aircraft.

Stage 5: The examinations

Once inside the aircraft the individual is subjected to a number of medical experiments. As we shall see in the subsequent chapters, the examinations are usually centered upon three aspects: the anatomy, emotions, and the psyche:

1. **Physiological Examinations:** Through a series of examinations and observations, the extraterrestrials explore the human anatomy.

2. **Emotional Responsiveness:** A common feature of extraterrestrial abductions is that these beings appear to be interested in human emotions and how we process them. This will be a recurring theme in the upcoming cases, and it appears that these visitors are particularly interested in how humans process fear and anxiety. In fact, these two emotions are elicited in the abductee through a series of telepathic images or messages and experiments.
3. **Human Consciousness:** The human psyche and consciousness are two prominent aspects of an alien abduction. These beings are undeniably as interested in the human psyche as they are in the anatomy. Following the encounter, many abductees report feeling a shift in their consciousness; thus, one must ask, how do these abductions affect the individual's consciousness and spirituality? More importantly, why are they so interested in the human soul?

Stage 6: The return

After the examinations are completed, the abductee is returned to the location from which they were abducted.

Stage 7: Missing time period

In the majority of abduction cases, following the return, individuals regularly report that they experience what is known as the missing time period. This phenomenon shows that these beings are capable of inducing an amnesiac state in the individual; in this state, the individual is unable to recall what had taken place in the previous hours. This phenomenon is usually the first indication that something sinister and preternatural has taken place.

Stage 8: Immediate and intermediate aftereffects

Following a close encounter with an extraterrestrial aircraft or entity, it is very common for individuals to develop symptoms and ailments, and this phenomenon has been reported for decades. Many military personnel who have had close encounters have also experienced these symptoms, and this has even prompted the Defense Intelligence Agency (DIA) to investigate these immediate and intermediate aftereffects. The DIA published a paper titled "Anomalous Acute and Subacute Field Effects on Human Biological Tissues" in 2009 as part of the Advanced

Aerospace Weapon System Applications program. The paper investi-
gates the injuries sustained following a close encounter with an "anomalous advanced aerospace system". The paper starts off by stating:

> Several years ago, three previous fit and active individuals experi-
> enced an anomalous ["irregular, incongruous and inconsistent with
> their domain"] aerospace-related event. Within 72 hours they suf-
> fered medical signs and symptoms [acute and subacute effects][47]

It then goes on to list the physical ailments that the individuals
experienced:

> They included almost immediate erythema (heat and redness) over
> exposed [to the presumed source of an electromagnetic radiation]
> skin, and varying degrees of the following as a function of their
> body-surface exposure times: fever, pain, headaches, numbness
> and paresthesia, malaise, diarrhea, loss of hair and alopecia, skin
> eruptions/boils, cardiac palpitations, beginnings of what were to
> become chronic headaches and symptoms of insomnia and other
> sleep and dream disturbances, moderate to occasional severe anx-
> iety and insomnia. Two of the persons also experienced photopho-
> bia (extreme sensitivity to light), dry and scratchy-stinging eyes,
> and extreme inflamed blood-shot sclerae (whites of the eyes) with
> soft tissue swelling of the eyelids. One of the three experienced
> moderate blood dyscrasia and signs of radiation illness, and over
> several years developed signs of malignant transformations.[48]

By now, the biophysical ailments are well understood by experts; however, the aircraft's propulsion system is not. This essentially means that
although we understand the symptoms and ailments reported, we do
not understand how these aircraft operate and thus cannot fully comprehend and explore the correlation between the two. It should be
noted that while this paper focused on close encounters of the first and
second kind, the symptoms listed are also experienced by abductees,

---

[47] Defense Intelligence Agency, "Anomalous Acute and subacute Field Effects on Human
Biological Tissues", *Defense Intelligence Agency*, December 2009, https://dia.mil/FOIA/
FOIA-Electronic-Reading-Room/FileId/170026/.
[48] Ibid.

and the symptoms are both physiological and psychological in nature. This paper consolidates two things: how detrimental these phenomena can be to the individual physically, and second, how profoundly traumatic these experiences can be.

Stage 9: Memory retrieval

At this point, the individual is still unable to recall what happened during the missing time period (the time of the abduction), and they have begun to experience immediate and intermediate aftereffects. As time passes, fragmented memories slowly start surfacing, and these are usually manifested as vivid and disjointed nightmares. As we will see in the upcoming cases, these nightmares usually consist of brief flashbacks and glimpses of what the extraterrestrial beings looked like and the experiments the individual was subjected to.

The ailments, missing time period, and fragmented memories are all signs that something unusual has occurred, and it is at this point that the individual becomes aware that something they cannot consciously recall has taken place. It is at this stage that many abductees reach out for help to further explore what is being kept from their conscious state. Many abductees choose to undergo hypnotic regression to recover their suppressed memories.

Stage 10: Awareness

In the final stage, more memories surface to the conscious state (either they surface naturally, or more commonly, through hypnotic regression). The individual is now fully aware that they have been abducted by an extraterrestrial entity.

▲ ▼ ▲

Hypnotic regression

The majority of alien abductions prove that these beings have the ability to manipulate the individual's memory, forcing them to either forget or block out the experience entirely. This is why it can take weeks or months for an individual to learn the full extent of their experience. In the coming chapters we will see how many abductees learn the full details of their abduction when they undergo hypnotic regression, but how precise is this technique? It must first be noted that details recalled under hypnosis are no more accurate than details recalled consciously. Second, hypnosis is not a memory-retrieval technique, which is why it is imperative that we do not rely solely on these memories when determining the credibility of a case. This is why other physical evidence is crucial as it will give us a more detailed picture of what has taken place. Aside from accessing suppressed memories, hypnotic regression is also used among abductees since they present trauma-related symptoms. As a matter of fact, several research studies have shown that hypnotic regression is extremely effective in treating trauma-related symptoms and disorders.[49,50]

▲ ▼ ▲

Polygraph tests

In the coming chapters, we will see how polygraph tests were commonly used to either substantiate alien abduction claims, or else debunk them. Although this instrument is commonly referred to as a lie detector, it does not actually detect lies; rather, it measures the individual's autonomic arousal (which consists of the heart and respiratory rate and skin conductivity). It is believed that if a person is being deceitful, the administrator will be able to detect it as there will be a change in the person's autonomic arousal.

At the start of the procedure, the administrator first carries out a pretest interview, during which they explain what a polygraph test consists of and what it is used for. They then proceed to take physiological readings from the individual. Following this, the administrator asks the individual to make factual statements about themselves, such as stating their name and date of birth. After this, they will ask them to purposefully lie. These measurements will be used as the baseline readings.

---

[49] Tudor Rotaru and Andrei Rusu, "A Meta-Analysis for the Efficacy of Hypnotherapy in Alleviating PTSD Symptoms", *International Journal of Clinical and Experiment Hypnosis*, 64(1) (2016).

[50] Institute of Medicine, Board on the Health of Select Populations, and Committee on the Assessment of Ongoing Efforts in the Treatment of Posttraumatic Stress Disorder, *Treatment for Post-Traumatic Stress Disorder in Military and Veteran Populations: Initial Assessment* (Washington, DC: National Academies Press, 2014).

Thereafter, the administrator starts asking the individual questions pertaining to the event.

Throughout the years, scientists have debated the credibility and accuracy of polygraph tests, and the reality is that one cannot conclusively determine if someone is lying or not—there is no one reading which reflects a lie. Moreover, the individual's physiological response is dependent on several factors, such as their levels of distress and anxiety, and it is crucial for this to be taken into consideration. For instance, if the individual is highly anxious, their readings are going to be higher than average. However, this does not prove that the person is lying. In the following chapters, I will not be relying solely on polygraph tests to determine the authenticity of a case, but I will be using it in conjunction with other pieces of evidence.

▲ ▼ ▲

What makes an alien abduction credible?

In the coming chapters, after recounting the individual's narrative I will explore the possible hypotheses. Many times, there are rational and prosaic explanations and thus the extraterrestrial hypothesis is not as plausible. In fact, while researching for this book, I came across many cases that were clearly a hoax. Having said that, I will not be including those cases in this book. In this book, I will be presenting the most credible and convincing cases that cannot be as easily refuted or debunked. Before doing so, I will first go over the factors which must be taken into consideration when assessing the authenticity of an alien abduction case.

Factor 1: The evidence

Something which I repeat quite often in this book is the importance of remaining factual and objective in our approach, and factuality requires evidence. The aforementioned immediate and intermediate aftereffects are significant pieces of evidence. If following the encounter, the individual's health abruptly deteriorates with no apparent cause, this is an indication that something obscure and bizarre might have taken place. Furthermore, other important pieces of evidence we look for include landing marks at the abduction site, analyses of soil, clothes, or other components related to the abduction, and corroborative UFO sightings.

Factor 2: Intention

The second factor is the person's intentions. The person's sincerity and attitude are integral indicators of the case's authenticity. Did the individual use the story to seek fame, publicity, and money? If so, this could be indicative of a hoax, especially if there is no substantial evidence to support their narrative. However, here I must make an important distinction: just because a case brings a person fame or money does not automatically imply that the case is a hoax. Success is not always predictable, and there will be cases where the person made money from their encounter but had substantial evidence to back up their claims. Everything must be taken into account.

Factor 3: The individual's health

Was the individual suffering from a psychopathology or a physical illness which could have caused hallucinations? Visual hallucinations can be caused by a variety of illnesses, including psychotic disorders and temporal lobe epilepsy. A thorough medical examination is required to rule out any medical conditions.

▲ ▼ ▲

Preternatural encounters cannot be scientifically proven, which makes it hard to conclusively determine whether an individual was indeed abducted or not. These three factors are critical in determining the authenticity of a case. We can only determine that the individual was abducted by an extraterrestrial entity if all rational explanations have been ruled out and if there is significant evidence which supports the extraterrestrial hypothesis. In each case, it is crucial to analyze every factor and piece of evidence, and then come up with an informed opinion. In some cases, the answer is clear cut, but many times it is not, and that is okay too. The phenomenon is complex, and we must accept its complexities and limitations; unanswered questions are inevitable.

CHAPTER 8

The abduction of a police officer

Date: 3rd December 1967
Location: Nebraska, United States

Credible eyewitnesses are crucial when determining the veracity of a UAP sighting or a close encounter. Due to their extensive training in observation and reporting, police officers make for exceptional and reliable eyewitnesses. Although just twenty-two years old at the time, Herbert Schirmer was a reputable police sergeant stationed in Nebraska. It was around 02:00 on the 3rd of December 1967 and Schirmer was on night duty, patrolling the streets and town of Ashland, Nebraska. As he was driving his truck along highway 6 on a cold December night, he observed flickering red lights to the right side of the road. He thought someone had been in an accident and needed help, so he pulled over to the side of the road. As he got closer to the lights, Schirmer noticed that they were coming from a disk-shaped aircraft hovering silently just a few feet above the ground. This, however, was only the beginning of what would be a harrowing time in Schirmer's life.

The encounter
3rd December 1967

As Schirmer noticed the flickering red lights to the side of the road, he halted at the intersection of highways 6 and 63 and turned on the truck's headlights, illuminating the immediate surroundings. It was then that he noticed that the lights were coming from a disk-shaped aircraft. The disk seemed like something out of a sci-fi movie, and initially he could not believe his eyes, so he rolled down his window and peered out to get a better look. He hoped it was just his mind playing tricks on him, but this was not the case. As he stuck his head out the truck's window, he could see that the metallic disk had a smooth, polished surface with flickering red lights around its rim. It was hovering completely silently, just a few feet off the ground, and after a few seconds, he heard a loud noise and saw a bright flame emerging from the disk's underside as it started ascending towards the sky. Within a few seconds, the disk shot up, disappearing in an instant. The next thing he recalled it was 03:00, and in his log book he wrote, "Saw a flying saucer at the junction of highways 6 and 63. Believe it or not!"[51] As we shall see, there was much more to the story than what he could consciously recall.

The aftermath

After his shift came to an end, Schirmer found it unusually difficult to fall asleep and described hearing a buzzing noise in his head. A few hours later, he discovered a two-inch red mark just below his left ear, and although he could not recall how he had gotten the mark, he did not think too much of it, and he certainly did not associate it with the previous night's sighting. That same day, he informed his superior of what he had seen, and together with a number of his colleagues, he went back to the landing site where they were able to locate metallic fragments scattered on the ground. Each fragment was about one centimeter long and had a bright aluminum color on one side and a dark black color on the other. This finding confirmed to his superior that Schirmer had indeed witnessed something unusual the previous night.

---

[51] Ralph Blum and Judy Blum, *Beyond Earth: Man's Contact with UFOs* (New York: Bantam Books, 1974), 110.

... small piece of metallic-appearing material which he did not rec-
ognize. This material, less than one centimeter long and paper thin
offered as possible residue left by the UFO. The chip of the material was black on one side, while the other surface had the bright
appearance of aluminum paint.[52]

Having said that, Schirmer was aware of the absurdity and prepos-
terousness of his story ... surely no one was going to believe that he
had seen an extraterrestrial aircraft. To prove he was telling the truth,
Schirmer asked to undergo a polygraph test. However, up until this
point, Schirmer was still not fully aware of everything that had taken
place that night—he thought that he had simply seen a UFO. The polygraph examination confirmed that Schirmer was being truthful, but
there was one major issue in his narrative—there was a twenty-minute
discrepancy which he could not account for. The missing time period,
the metallic fragments at the site, and the physiological symptoms he
experienced were indicative that something bizarre had happened, and
thus, the Condon Committee initiated a full investigation into the case.

> A state trooper, on duty since 5 p.m., was cruising the outskirts of
> his small midwestern town alone at 02:30. He reported a saucer-like
> object landed or hovered over the highway 40 ft in front of him. The
> object departed straight upward at high speed. The trooper could
> not account for a 20-min period during which he assumed he must
> have been near the UFO.[53]

▲ ▼ ▲

The investigation

Mr. Schirmer felt perhaps he had not been conscious during a period of
approximately 20 minutes while he was observing the UFO. He had a
feeling of paralysis at the time, and felt funny, weak, sick and nervous
when he returned to the police station. The patrolman seemed quite
sincere in presenting his report.[54]

---

[52] Edward Condon, *Final Report of the Scientific Study of Unidentified Flying Objects*
(New York: Bantam, 1969), Case 42.
[53] Condon, *Final Report of the Scientific Study of Unidentified Flying Objects*, Case 42.
[54] Ibid.

Two months after the encounter, the Condon Committee set up a meeting between Schirmer, Leo Sprinkle, a psychologist at the University of Wyoming, and Bill Wlaskin, a chief police investigator. The professionals were especially interested in the missing time period—the fact that Schirmer could not consciously recall the entirety of his encounter suggested that there were more details which were buried in his subconscious, making him an ideal candidate to undergo hypnotic regression.

Hypnotic regression

Schirmer agreed to undergo hypnotic regression with experienced hypnotherapist Loring Williams. The details which Schirmer uncovered were deeply disconcerting. Under hypnotic regression, Schirmer revealed that upon reaching the intersection, he noticed what appeared to be a disk-shaped aircraft hovering silently only a few feet above the ground. More specific than what he had consciously recalled, Schirmer described the disk as having an oval, football-like shape and a silver, shiny metallic surface. The flickering, bright red lights he had seen from the highway were around the disk's perimeter, and beneath it was a bright silver glow. Schirmer went on to say that shortly after he arrived, a landing gear protruded from beneath the disk as it made a smooth landing on the ground.

Schirmer attempted to start his truck in a panic, but he was unable to do so, as if someone or something was impeding on his ability to move. Just a few feet away from him, he noticed the dark silhouette of a creature emerging from beneath the disk. As his eyes adjusted to the bright glow emanating from the disk, he noticed that the silhouette was now approaching him, making him feel inexplicably uneasy. All he knew was that he needed to get away as quickly as possible, but he had no control over his body. Schirmer could see the creature more clearly through the rolled-down truck windows, and its sinister appearance proved that it was undoubtedly an extraterrestrial creature.

The creature had a disproportionately shaped head that was longer and thinner than a human's and stood at around five foot tall. Its skin was a grayish-white color and had a tiny slit for a mouth and a completely flat nose that was only barely visible. The eyes were slanted and lacked eyelids and lashes, but interestingly, the pupils fluctuated in size and shape like a camera lens. The alien was dressed in gloves, boots, and a light-filled silver garment that covered his head, just like a helmet. On the left side of the head was a small device similar to an antenna and on the left side of the chest was an emblem of a winged serpent. Fearing for his life, Schirmer tried to withdraw the revolver from his holster, but the being reactively raised an object that released a green gas, covering his vehicle entirely. The alien neared even closer and pulled out another small instrument and pointed it towards him, and at that moment, Schirmer saw a bright white light and lost consciousness. Back in the clinical room, Schirmer was distraught and Williams had to repeatedly reassure him of his safety.

> Williams: Are you afraid?
> Schirmer: You're damn right. My hand is shaking.
> Williams: Why don't you start your cruiser and leave?
> Schirmer: I am being prevented. Something in my mind …
> I wanna go home. Lord! Oh no! Oh no![55]

Still under a hypnotic trance, Schirmer continued to relive the night of the 3rd of December. After he regained consciousness, he saw the creature beside him, grabbing him by the shoulder and pressing the side of his neck. This was assumingly how he had gotten the red mark he discovered the following day. Schirmer was in a complete daze, not knowing whether what he was experiencing was a dream or reality, but as the being squeezed his shoulder, he suddenly realized that this was reality and there was no way of escaping it. The door to the driver's seat opened and he locked eyes with the being. As the two locked eyes with one another, the creature pointed to the nearby power plant and simultaneously, Schirmer heard a foreign voice in his head, asking him if he was the watchman of the nearby water reservoir and whether this power plant was the only power source in the area.

The alien was now walking back toward the disk and motioned for Schirmer to follow him. Beneath the disk was a ladder which led to the inside, and as they approached the disk, Schirmer once again described the lack of control he felt over his body—someone or something was controlling his movements. Inside the disk was a room about six feet high and twenty to twenty-six feet in diameter, with fluorescent strips attached to the ceiling emitting a bright light. There were portholes all around the room and attached to one of the walls was a control panel with two chairs behind it and a large vision screen above.

---

[55] Blum and Blum, *Beyond Earth*, 112.

Schirmer recalled that the being was communicating with him both tele-pathically and verbally. He described its voice as coming from inside its body rather than its mouth and compared it to someone who speaks in broken English.

On the display screen was an image of an aircraft which was simi-lar to the one they were on but smaller. The creature explained how this was an observational aircraft and was used for surveillance, recon-naissance, and transmitting pictures. The being pressed a button on the control panel, and the screen's view changed to show the outside of the disk they were on. Outside the disk were two creatures similar to the one he was communicating with, walking back and forth, patrol-ling. The being pressed a third button, and the screen now showed three differently shaped aircraft against a black, speckled background. A fourth button was pressed, and the creature explained to Schirmer that the cigar-shaped object on the screen was the mothership—the main aircraft.

Still under a hypnotic trance, Schirmer continued describing his close encounter. Schirmer inquired about their mode of communication, and the creature told him that they had a device on board which allowed them to speak any language on Earth. He was also told that they are from a nearby galaxy and have several bases on Earth, all located under-water. The bases are located off the coast of Florida, in the polar-region, off the coast of Argentina, and a fourth one in an unspecified location beneath the ocean. Other planets in the Milky Way contain similar alien bases as well, though the creature did not elaborate any further.

The conversation was then centered upon the aircraft's propulsion system. Schirmer observed how there was no visible propulsion engine, and the being confirmed that they use a reversible electro-magnetic propulsion system, which allows the aircraft to generate its own gravi-tational field. With this gravitational field, the aircraft can bend space-time, allowing it to travel great distances in a shorter period of time. In the middle of the room was a rotor that was attached to two large cylin-drical columns—these were the propulsion system's reactors. Inside these reactors, the electro-magnetism is reversed, which then creates the aircraft's gravitational field. The aircraft indisputably seemed more sophisticated and advanced than any terrestrial aircraft he was aware of. With that said, the being explained how one of their aircraft was once intercepted by the Air Force's radar, but in order to prevent any useful technology from being recovered from the crash site, the aircraft is equipped with a device that self-destructs the aircraft before it hits the ground.

The being then proceeded to demonstrate to Schirmer how the aircraft reversed electromagnetism by using electricity from nearby power lines. On the screen Schirmer could see an antenna emerge from the disk's exterior and was aimed at a nearby power line. In a short while, a burst of white electricity soared in the direction of the antenna, and Schirmer saw one of the gauges on the control panel spike, signifying a surge in power within the disk. Aside from the power lines, the disk also retrieved energy from water, which is why the being had inquired about the water reservoir. Before Schirmer was escorted back outside, he was instructed to keep his account of the close encounter brief and to only report seeing a disk in the sky, but nothing more than that. Schirmer was also told that he would see them on two more occasions, but he made no further reports in subsequent years.

Once Schirmer was escorted back to his truck, the landing gear retracted back into the disk and a bright reddish-orange light emitted from beneath the aircraft as it shot up toward the sky, disappearing in an instant.

> Dr. Sprinkle expressed the opinion that the trooper believed in the reality of the events he described.[56]

▲ ▼ ▲

In the days following the encounter, Schirmer experienced a radical deterioration in his health. He started experiencing psychological distress, which was so intense that it was causing him severe headaches. Upon his return to Nebraska from Laramie, Wyoming, Schirmer was given a promotion, making him the youngest police chief in the Midwest. This position, however, was short-lived; due to the psychological distress he was experiencing, he willingly resigned just two months later.

> I kept wondering what had happened that night. My headaches were getting pretty fierce; I was gobbling down aspirin like it

---

[56] Condon, *Final Report of the Scientific Study of Unidentified Flying Objects*, Case 42.

was popcorn. You can't be a good policeman if you have personal problems.[57]

Once the investigation came to an end, the Condon Committee concluded that the case was a hoax. The Committee stated that the lack of physical evidence, the interviews they held with Schirmer, and the psychological tests they performed all indicated that Schirmer had not actually been abducted by an extraterrestrial entity.

> Evaluation of psychological assessment tests, the lack of any evidence and interviews with the patrolman left project staff with no confidence that the trooper's reported UFO experience was physically real.[58]

Hypotheses

Hypothesis #1: A misidentification

Is it possible that Schirmer's sighting of a disk-shaped aircraft was a misidentification of a conventional aircraft, such as a helicopter? There are numerous reasons as to why I don't find this to be a plausible explanation. First, this hypothesis requires us to assume that Schirmer's reporting of the aircraft's features was completely inaccurate, and realistically, it is hard to believe that Schirmer would have confused an oval-shaped aircraft with such unconventional characteristics to a helicopter or any other terrestrial aircraft. Second, this hypothesis does not account for the immediate and intermediate aftereffects reported by Schirmer; it is worth repeating that he experienced such a severe deterioration in his health that he had to resign from his recently promoted position.

Hypothesis #2: A hoax

Is it possible that the Condon Committee's conclusion on the case is correct and Schirmer made up the entire story? To consolidate their theory, the Committee made reference to psychological tests which Schirmer

---

[57] Blum and Blum, *Beyond Earth*, 110.
[58] Condon, *Final Report of the Scientific Study of Unidentified Flying Objects*, Case 42.

underwent, and the fact that he performed poorly on them supported their conclusion. However, the assessments in question refer to conceptual thinking and word association tests, and although he did indeed score low on the tests, they do not reflect whether Schirmer was being truthful or not. It is also incorrect for the Condon Committee to state there was no physical evidence when metallic fragments were located at the site. Another factor which does not support this hypothesis is the fact that Schirmer did not gain anything from this story. In actual fact, he had to resign from his position due to the psychological distress he was experiencing. Why would he have fabricated a story and jeopardize his career?

Hypothesis #3: The extraterrestrial hypothesis

The third hypothesis we shall explore is the extraterrestrial hypothesis. This hypothesis is supported by physical evidence as well as the fact that Schirmer's description of the aircraft and how it operates corresponds to our current understanding of how UAP operate. The first factor which supports this hypothesis is the physical evidence: the immediate and intermediate aftereffects Schirmer experienced, and the metallic fragments he located at the landing site. It should be noted that the discovery of the metallic fragments directly contradicts the Condon Committee's claim that there was no physical evidence to back up Schirmer's testimony.

What intrigues me the most about this case is the fact that Schirmer's description of how the aircraft works, as well as the details that emerged from his conversation with the entity, all align with the knowledge we currently have on UAP and how they operate. For instance, Schirmer was told that the beings have underwater bases, naturally implying that the aircraft possess trans-medium capabilities. This is consistent with one of the five observables as well as Commander David Fravor's testimony of the USS *Nimitz* encounter, in which the tic-tac-shaped UFO outmaneuvered Commander Fravor's fighter jet in the sky and proceeded to plunge into the ocean, where it traveled at twice the speed of the Navy's fastest submarine. Furthermore, Schirmer stated that the aircraft contains two large cylindrical columns which are the propulsion system's reactors, inside which electromagnetism is reversed and the aircraft's own gravitational field is produced. This is consistent with the idea that UAP utilize an anti-gravitational propulsion system. I also have to emphasize the striking similarity between this description and Bob Lazar's testimony.

▲ ▼ ▲

Conclusion

As time has passed and our understanding of UAP has improved, we have gained a better understanding of the phenomenon and how these aircraft operate. These discoveries, made decades after Schirmer's experience, are startlingly correspondent, and this precision is unlikely to have been just a coincidence. Could Schirmer's story have been so accurate because he was telling the truth and was indeed abducted by an extraterrestrial entity? Although the Committee concluded that Schirmer fabricated the entire story, we must be cognizant of all the factors, and must analyze and scrutinize them carefully using the information we have available to us nowadays. If it was the case that Schirmer fabricated the story, then he certainly carried out extensive and accurate research.

CHAPTER 9

The Travis Walton experience

Date: 5th November 1975
Location: Arizona, United States

It was Wednesday, the 5th of November 1975. Travis Walton, then a twenty-two-year-old forestry worker, was working at the Apache-Sitgreaves National Forest in Snowflake, Arizona, alongside his colleagues, Mike Rogers, Allen Dalis, John Goulette, Dwayne Smith, Kenneth Peterson, and Steve Pierce. The forestry company had a tree-thinning contract, and the day was as ordinary as any other; by 18:00, as the sun began to set, they loaded their equipment onto the truck and began their hour-and-a-half drive back home. However, the day would end in an unpredictable way—within a few hours Travis would go missing after being "struck" by a flying disk and would only return several days later, claiming that he had been abducted by aliens. What follows is the fascinating story of Travis Walton. Over four decades later, individuals and researchers are still debating and discussing the authenticity of the case, some claiming it was a well-planned hoax and an attempt for fame and money, while others believe it was a genuine alien abduction case.

▲ ▼ ▲

The encounter
5th November 1975

As the sun began to set at the Apache-Sitgreaves National Forest, Travis, Mike, Allen, John, Dwayne, Kenneth, and Steve started packing up their equipment and loading it onto their truck. Shortly into the hour-and-a-half drive back home to Snowflake, one of the men noticed a bright light in the sky which started moving effortlessly and swiftly from side to side. They rolled down the windows to get a better view of it and were surprised at how agile it was maneuvering; it was just like a laser point. They started speculating on what the light was: they first thought it was the sun, but it had set just a few minutes prior. They then debated every possible explanation, from meteorites to military aircraft, but none fit with what they were seeing.

The men continued to stare outside the truck's window as the light continued to maneuver and shine through the forest trees. They then noticed that the light was getting closer and were able to discern its characteristics—the light was, in fact, a disk-shaped aircraft with a dome structure on its top and a flange around its center. They estimated it to be around twenty feet wide and eight feet thick and saw it was emitting a warm yellow glow. It had a completely smooth surface with no visible windows or portholes; they also noticed how it was hovering and maneuvering completely silently. Back inside the truck there was a mixture of uneasiness and excitement as the disk continued to inch closer to the vehicle. The disk was now hovering just a few feet away, around twenty feet above a slash pile. They stopped the truck to get an unobstructed view of it, and for some reason or another, Travis pushed open the door and dashed toward the clearing where the disk was hovering above. In subsequent interviews Travis stated that he was acting on an "urge."

As he started running towards the disk, his colleagues shouted for him to return, and while he did stop midway and deliberated, he chose to continue on. His friends could only look ahead and watch as things unfolded. Travis was now in the middle of the clearing, standing just a few feet away from the disk; from that close proximity he started hearing a frequency being emitted from it, and he compared the noise to several turbine generators operating simultaneously. The intensity of the frequency started to rise and at that moment Travis realized that this had been a terrible idea and needed to return back to the truck.

He crouched behind a rock and was seized with fear, for he did not know what the disk was or where it came from. Just as he decided to turn and start running back, his body enfeebled, and he dropped to the ground. This was Travis's final recollection of what happened that day.

> His colleagues, on the other hand, saw a different sight: as Travis started running back toward the truck, the disk emitted a bolt of energy (similar to lightning) and struck his body, throwing him several feet off the ground. Kenneth Peterson, 25: I saw a bluish light come from the machine and Travis went flying—like he'd touched a hot wire.
>
> Alan Dalis, 21: It sent out a blue ray, and the last we saw of Travis was his silhouette outlined, arms outstretched. We couldn't believe what was happening—the horror was unreal![59]

As Travis lay unconscious on the ground, the group started fearing for their own safety, so they dashed back into the truck and sped away from the scene. Once they were some miles away, reality sank in: they had left Travis behind and he was in dire need of medical attention. They pulled the vehicle to the side of the road and regained their composure. Everyone was in complete shock; not only had they seen a flying saucer, but it had seemingly electrocuted Travis. As the men discussed their next course of action, they noticed a bright light ascending from the distance, contrasting with the now dark sky. The light proceeded to shoot up toward the sky at an incredible speed, disappearing in an instant. Was this light the disk they had seen just a few minutes earlier?

It had now dawned on them that they needed to get back to Travis immediately, but as they drove back to the site, he was nowhere to be found. They turned on the truck's headlights and torches but alas, there were no signs of his presence—there were no marks, no trails, nothing. It was also getting colder and darker, and they needed to involve the police, so they drove back to Snowflake and dialed the police station from the nearest phone booth. Prior to that, they had agreed between them that it was best to initially omit the flying disk from the narrative to ensure that the police would take them seriously, and shortly after Ken spoke with Deputy Sheriff Chuck Ellison, they met up with him at a designated location and told him the full story. Whether he believed

---

[59] "Arizona Man Captured by UFO", *The National Enquirer*, December 16, 1975.

them or not, a person had gone missing and the likelihood of someone surviving in the forest in cold temperatures was dwindling as time
passed by.

The search

The six men told Deputy Sheriff Chuck Ellison the entire story, who
then notified County Deputy Glen Flake of the situation. Before initiat-
ing a search, Deputy Sheriff Ellison went to Travis's residence to ensure
that he was not there, and once he confirmed his absence, he informed
Sheriff Marlin Gillespie to make a missing person report. Together with
Undersheriff Ken Coplan, Sheriff Gillespie went to the alleged abduction site where they questioned each of the six men individually. They
searched the area as thoroughly as they could, but it was dark, and their
resources were limited. They were unable to find Travis or any hints
of his presence, which raised further suspicion to an already dubious
situation.

Now that the night had set in and several hours had passed, they
needed to inform Travis's family, so together with Undersheriff Coplan,
Mike, Travis's longtime friend and manager, drove to his mother's
house in Bear Springs. As Mary Kellet opened the door, Mike informed
her of what had happened, and surprisingly, she did not seem to be
overly alarmed about the situation. Her reaction, or lack thereof, raised
more questions: was Mary expecting the visit? Did she know where
Travis was or what his plans were?

> When Rogers told the mother what had happened, she did not act
> very surprised.[60]

The following day they planned on returning to the site to continue
looking for Travis, and everyone gathered at Mary's house early in
the morning. Prior to setting out for the search, Travis's brothers Duane
and Don questioned the six men about what had happened the day
before. Understandably they struggled to fathom their story, and the
situation quickly escalated and became tense as they accused the men

---

[60] Philip J. Klass, *UFOs: The Public Deceived* (New York: Prometheus Books, 1983), 162.

of foul play. Back at the forest, a search and rescue team was formed, which consisted of half a dozen officers on horseback and a search and rescue helicopter with spotters on board. Later that day, while everyone was looking for any hints of Travis, Mary made another suspicious remark—she told the sheriff that the search was futile and that they would not find Travis because he was not here on Earth: "I don't think there is any use of looking any further. He's not around here. I don't think he's on this Earth." Many have argued that Mary's disposition to the situation indicated that she was involved in a hoax, and I can understand why so many have come to such a conclusion. It is hard to believe that if someone went missing, their mother would so readily accept that they had been abducted by aliens.

As the hours went by, word started to spread, and it did not take long for the media to pick up on the story and arrive at the scene. Among the reporters was William Spaulding from the *Ground Saucer Watch*, who spoke with Duane at length about the situation and alien abductions in general. Spaulding informed Duane that upon Travis's return, it was imperative that he got medically assessed. With that being said, Sanford Lake, the town marshal did not entertain the extraterrestrial hypothesis for a moment. He was certain that this was either a prank, or the men were responsible for his disappearance. For this reason, a few days later, he asked them to undergo a polygraph test, which was administered by Cy Gilson from the Department of Public Safety. Gilson posed Allen, John, Dwayne, Kenneth, Steve, and Mike the following four questions:

1) Had they caused Travis harm?
2) Had Travis been injured by one of the crew members?
3) Was Travis buried in Turkey Springs (the forest where Travis had disappeared)?
4) Were they being truthful about seeing a flying disk on the day and around the time of Travis's disappearance?

John, Dwayne, Kenneth, Steve, and Mike's results were conclusive and corroborated the testimony they had given. Allen's test, however, was inconclusive. Five men had now given the same testimony and had each passed the polygraph test.

> Each of the six men answered "no" to questions 1, 2 and 3, and they
> each answered "yes" to question 4. The test results were conclusive

on Goulette, Smith, Peterson, Rogers and Pierce. The test results on Dalis were inconclusive.

Based on the polygraph chart tracing, it is the opinion of this examiner that Goulette, Smith, Peterson, Rogers and Pierce were being truthful when they answered these relevant questions.

These polygraph examinations prove that these five men did see some object that they believe to be a UFO, and that Travis Walton was not injured or murdered by any of these men on that Wednesday. If an actual UFO did not exist and the UFO is a man-made hoax, five of these men had no prior knowledge of a hoax. No such determination can be made of the sixth man, whose test results were inconclusive.[61]

At this point, Travis had been missing for five days, and if he was indeed stranded in the forest with no water, food, or shelter in the freezing temperatures, the likelihood of finding him alive was extremely slim. To everyone's surprise, on the fifth day of the investigation, a phone call was made late at night to Travis's sister's house—it was Travis, and he had returned.

▲ ▼ ▲

The return
10th November 1975

It was Monday the 10th of November around midnight when a phone call was made to Alison, Travis's sister, at her home. Grant, Alison's husband, answered the phone, but the family had recently been receiving several prank calls from people claiming to be Travis. Just as Grant was about to hang up, he heard a faint voice and recognized it as Travis's, who told him that he "had been brought back" and was in a telephone booth in Heber. Grant immediately called Duane and they rushed to Heber, where they found Travis in one of three phonebooths, lying on the ground, shivering, looking depleted and in a state of shock.

They helped him into the truck, but Travis was in great distress and was unable to form coherent sentences. He kept repeating that "they"

[61] Jerome, Clark, *The UFO Book: Encyclopedia of the Extraterrestrial* (Detroit, MI: Visible Ink Press, 1998), 663.

were awful and described them as having white skin with massive, bulging eyes. He did not elaborate who "they" were. He also presumed that he had only been missing for a few hours and was unaware of the fact that it had actually been five days. Once they arrived home, they helped him undress, and Duane noticed a red spot on the inside of his right elbow. Moreover, when they weighed him, Travis noted that he had lost ten pounds. Keeping in mind the conversation he had had with Spaulding, Duane collected the clothes he was wearing and placed them in a paper bag. He also kept a urine sample.

A few hours later, an anonymous tip informed the sheriff's office that Travis had returned, and upon hearing this, the sheriff ordered a number of officers to watch the highway, and he himself drove over to Travis's house. Having said that, Travis was still in shock and not in a fit state to be interrogated, so Duane informed the sheriff that he had not heard from Travis and that his source was most likely mistaken. Duane knew however that it would only be a matter of hours before people would start showing up at the house, so he thought it would be best to take Travis to his house in Phoenix where he would be able to recover without any disturbances or pressure from the press and the police. The first night was unsettling and restless for Travis: he experienced vivid dreams which consisted of ominous creatures with large, bulging eyes, staring down at him.

The following morning Duane contacted Spaulding to inform him of Travis's return and to inquire as to what they should do next. Spaulding offered the organization's support, and he recommended them to Dr. Lester Steward who was a consultant for *Ground Saucer Watch*. Upon their arrival at the office, Travis and Duane were thrown off by a plaque at the door which stated that Dr. Steward was a hypnotherapist. During the examination itself, Duane did the majority of the talking as Travis was visibly distressed and in shock. Dr. Steward then performed a brief physical assessment and noted the red mark at the elbow and recommended further tests. While he was gathering the necessary information and making phone calls, Duane grew impatient, so they left the office and went back to his house in Glendale.

Throughout the day Duane started receiving phone calls from people asking about Travis's whereabouts. One of the callers was Coral Lorenzen, the secretary treasurer at *APRO*, the Aerial Phenomena Research Organization. Lorenzen was very understanding of the situation and she agreed that Travis needed immediate medical assistance, and thus she arranged for Dr. Howard Kandell and Dr. Joseph Sault to do a house visit and assess Travis. Just hours later, Lorenzen was in talks with *The National Enquirer*—in exchange for exclusive coverage, the newspaper would pay for all the medical expenses the investigation required. A urine analysis was performed, and it was discovered that there were no acetones in the urine. This was a significant discovery: when the body goes without food for twenty-four to forty-eight hours, it starts breaking down fat stores, releasing ketones in the urine. This indicated that Travis had received some form of nutrition in the past few days.

At this point, the sheriff insisted on speaking with Travis that same night, and he agreed, as long as he did not disclose his location to anyone. Later on that night, Sheriff Gillespie asked Travis a number of questions, and he noted that he looked agitated and shocked. The sheriff also insisted that Travis undergoes a polygraph test a few days later, but Travis did not show up as he stated he was not prepared to face the press. Despite this, he was speaking with *The National Enquirer* at the same time, which seemed contradictory. A few days later, as reporters found out about Travis's location, he and Duane moved to a room at the Scottsdale Sheraton Inn. There, Duane spoke with *The Arizona Daily Star*, with the headlines reading "Man Says Brother Spent 5 Days on UFO." In the article, Duane stated:

> He was on a UFO for five days and did have some contact with alien beings. I'm not a UFO buff and neither is my brother. I'm convinced he's telling the truth. He's never lied in his life, never even played a practical joke.[62]

The National Enquirer interview

The interview with *The National Enquirer* was held on the 13th of November. On the day, Travis and Duane met with Lorenzen from *APRO*, Paul Jenkins from *The National Enquirer*, as well as Dr. James Harder, a hypnotherapist. In this introductory meeting, Dr. Harder talked with Travis at length and tried to deduce whether he was susceptible to hypnotic regression, which he was. As part of the feature,

[62] "Man Says Brother Spent 5 Days on UFO", *The Arizona Daily Star*, November 12, 1971.

Jenkins wished for Travis to undergo a polygraph test as this would validate his story even further. The test was administered by Dr. John McCarthy, who concluded that Travis was not being truthful. With that being said, this finding and McCarthy's observations were omitted from the article.

> It was obvious during the examination that he was deliberately attempting to distort his respiration pattern. Based on his reactions on all charts, it is the opinion of this examiner that Walton, in concert with others, is attempting to perpetrate a UFO hoax and that he has not been on any spacecraft.[63]

To assess the credibility of the case, Lorenzen invited three psychiatrists: Dr. Jean Rosenbaum, Dr. Beryl Rosenbaum, and Dr. Warren Gorman. From their assessment, they concluded that this story was not a hoax, but they did not believe that Travis had been abducted by an extraterrestrial entity either. They believed that there was a rational explanation for this, and Dr. Rosenbaum proposed that Travis had suffered from a transitory psychotic episode and amnesia: his experience was the result of a psychotic episode and his inability to recall what had happened during the five days was a symptom of amnesia. This explanation, however, did not explain how Travis would have managed to survive five days in the forest.

> Our conclusion—which is absolute—is that this young man is not lying—that there is no collusion, no attempt to hoax … [Dr. Rosenbaum goes on to add that] he [Travis] really believes he was abducted by a UFO. But my evaluation of the boy's story is that … it was all in his own mind. I feel that he suffered from a combination of imagination and amnesia, a transitory psychosis—that he did not go on a UFO, but simply was wandering around during the period of his disappearance. But I'm unable to account for five witnesses having [telling] the same basic story and passing lie detector tests about it.[64]

---

[63] Jerome Clark, *High Strangeness: UFOs from 1960 through 1979*, (Detroit, MI: Omnigraphics Inc, 1996), 554.
[64] Klass, *UFOs*, 174.

Hypnotic regression

Following his return, Travis reportedly started experiencing vivid and recurring nightmares which consisted of ominous, bizarre creatures with large, dark eyes. In the introductory meeting, Dr. Harder surmised that Travis was a good candidate for hypnotic regression, and thus recommended that he undergoes hypnosis to explore what was being concealed from his conscious state. Once Dr. Harder guided Travis into a calm hypnotic trance, they went back to the 5th of November.

Travis recalled that as the sun started to set, they started loading the equipment onto the truck and started their drive back home. At that point it must have been around 18:00, and shortly into the hour and a half drive, one of his colleagues noticed a bright light in the sky that began to maneuver erratically as it continually got closer to the vehicle. As it approached their position and was close enough for them to observe its characteristics, they were surprised to see that the light was a disk-shaped aircraft with a dome structure on top. It was estimated to be around twenty feet wide and eight feet thick. It had a flange around its center and a completely smooth surface with no visible windows or portholes. It emitted a warm yellow glow as it hovered and maneuvered completely silently. After a few moments, the disk glided toward a clearing where it continued to hover above a slash pile. With the truck parked, Travis described how he felt an inexplicable urge to run towards it and get closer to it. He opened the truck's door and sprinted towards the clearing as his friends shouted for him to turn back. He was now close enough to hear a frequency being emitted from the disk which instilled fear in him. Travis ducked behind a rock to plan his next move, and as he began to run back towards the truck, he was hit by a burst of energy that paralyzed his entire body, causing him to fall to the ground, losing consciousness.

He was unaware of how much time had passed, and when he opened his eyes, he found himself in what seemed to be a hospital room. The bright fluorescent strips lit up the room and he felt something was being pressed down onto his chest. As he looked down towards his abdomen, he saw a grey colored instrument curved around his body, covering from his armpits down to the abdomen. He also sensed the presence of someone behind him, and as he looked around, he saw three creatures, one to his left and two to his right. The beings stood at roughly five foot tall and had a miniscule, childlike stature. They had large, disproportionate heads with dark, bulging, brown eyes and large irises. They did not have any brows or eyelashes and had small, crinkled ear lobes with a tiny nose and a slit for a mouth. They were dressed in a one-piece orange overall and Travis further noted how their skin seemed somewhat translucent and soft.

> I thought I was in a hospital. I was lying on a table on my back, and these figures were standing over me. It was weird. They weren't human—they were creatures. They looked like well-developed fetuses to me.[65]

Travis could only look around him as he was constricted by the instrument wrapped around his body. With the three grotesque creatures before him, he felt threatened and instinctively stood up and pushed the two creatures to his right away from him. As his hands touched their body, he confirmed that their skin was indeed soft and light. The device wrapped around his body fell to the floor, but he felt too lethargic to stand up. In a panic he looked around the room and saw several instruments on a metallic counter. The three creatures simply stared at him with their arms outstretched as though they were signaling for him to calm down. As reality started to set in, he realized that he was trapped in a room with three aliens, and the only way out was through the door which they were blocking. On the metallic counter he grabbed the cylindrical tube and hit it on the surface in an attempt to break it and sharpen its edges. However, regardless of how hard he hit it, it would not break. Travis tried to devise a plan, and just before he moved forward to barge through them, the three creatures exited the room and hurried down the corridor.

He breathed a sigh of relief and finally had the chance to regain his composure and take in his surroundings. The room was oddly small, clearly not designed for human adults, with convexly curved walls and a triangular ceiling only seven feet high. The surfaces on both the wall and the floor curved into each other and even the table and bench came to a curve. He further noticed how the metallic surfaces were completely smooth with no apparent bolts, screws, or welds. On the counter from which he took the cylinder were several other instruments, but he had no idea what their function was.

---

[65] "Arizona Man Captured by UFO", *The National Enquirer*, December 16, 1975.

Travis was unaware of where he was, and he desperately wanted to get out and return back home. As he looked out the door, he saw a narrow hallway, just three feet wide which came to a curve at the end. He walked down silently and noticed another narrow, dimly lit passageway, but it led in the same direction the three beings went, so he turned and went the opposite way. As he continued to walk on, he noticed a room and as he entered, he noticed it was structured similarly to the one he was previously in. The room was completely bare except for an empty chair in the center, which was slightly tilted. From afar he noticed that one of its arms had a lever and several buttons beneath it. Curiously, Travis started walking towards it, and simultaneously the room started getting darker and white specks covered the walls and floor. Travis stopped and walked backwards, and as he did, the effect diminished. He walked towards the chair once again and the effect returned. As he stood next to the chair he noticed that on the right arm was a five-inch green screen with twenty-five colored buttons beneath it. The buttons were assorted in five vertical rows, each with a different color: red, yellow, green, blue and violet. On the screen were multiple black lines which intersected each other at different angles.

Intrigued, Travis pressed one of the green buttons and instantly, the lines on the screen started moving collectively. He pressed a different button, and the lines changed direction. He then pushed the lever forward and as he did, the white specks covering the room started moving downward, making him feel disorientated. He pushed the lever to the opposite direction, and the specks moved accordingly. Aside from the white specks he also started seeing the colorful band of the Milky Way and breathtaking nebulous clouds. It was at that moment that he realized that the specks were stars and that he was in outer space. Travis described it as though he was sitting on a chair suspended in space. After a few moments, he stood up and began walking backwards towards the door, the specks fading away simultaneously.

Travis heard a noise coming from outside the room, and as he looked, he saw what seemed to be a human being approaching him. He was stunned at this and was unsure whether it was indeed a human or not, but it had anthropomorphic and masculine features. The being was around six foot tall and had proportionate bodily features with medium-length blond hair and hazel colored eyes. He had a tanned complexion and wore a blue, tight-fitted suit with boots and a transparent helmet. The man gestured for Travis to follow him, and as he started walking down the hallway, Travis tried asking him questions, but frustratingly, the man simply dismissed him. He grabbed Travis by the hand and guided him down the corridor where they entered a small, empty room. Inside it a doorway opened, letting warm light and fresh air in. They walked down a ramp that led to a larger room, and as they walked down, Travis noticed that they had exited the aircraft as now he could see the disk's curved shape and exterior metallic surface. In this large hangar were three other disks which had similar features to the one he was in but were significantly smaller. Travis continued to ask him questions, but the being continued to ignore him.

Travis was led into another room, and inside it was three other beings, all with the same human-like appearance. Two of them appeared to have masculine features, while the third appeared to have feminine features. The three beings wore the same attire and had the same complexion, but they were not wearing the transparent helmet. The room was also akin to the one he was originally in, with a rounded table in the center. One of the men and the woman approached Travis and grabbed him by the arm and started pushing him gently onto the table. The woman held a mask which looked like an oxygen mask but instead of the tubes at the end, it had a sphere attached to it. Travis tried resisting their force, but the woman pressed the mask against his face and his consciousness started to fade. That was the last memory Travis recalled. As he regained consciousness, he found himself on the cold pavement in Heber, Arizona. He was unaware of what had happened or for how long he had been missing. He felt incredibly lethargic, and he staggered until he found a phone booth, which he used to call his sister.

From that day forward, Travis's life would never be the same again; in the subsequent days he would experience flashbacks and vivid nightmares. When he did manage to get some rest, he would wake up in a pool of sweat. The details recounted under hypnotic regression are certainly intriguing, however; aside from his experience on the empty chair, he did not recall being subjected to any other experiments. Decades later, Travis still recounts his experience vividly and has spoken publicly about it on numerous occasions. His autobiographical book, *The Walton Experience*, was also adapted into a well-received movie, *A Fire in the Sky*.

▲ ▼ ▲

A year later ...

The moment Travis returned, many expressed their opinion as to whether this was a genuine alien abduction case or not. A year down the line, he himself, Duane, and their mother underwent a polygraph test, which was administered by George Pfeifer. This test must be criticized for the simple reason that the questions were formulated by Dr. Leonard Sprinkle and Jim Lorenzen, and thus there was bound to be bias since they were both active members in the UFO community. Needless to say, all three individuals passed the polygraph test. The report reads as follows:

> It is the opinion of this examiner that Duane Walton has answered all questions truthfully according to what he believes to be the truth regarding this incident, and he has not attempted to be deceptive in any area ...
>
> After a careful analysis of the polygraphs produced, there are no areas left unresolved and it is the opinion of this examiner that Travis Walton has answered all questions in a manner that he himself is convinced to be the truth regarding the incident commencing 11-5-75.[66]

▲ ▼ ▲

The samples

Interestingly enough, in 2017, forty-two years after Travis's encounter at the Apache-Sitgreaves National Forest, *Frontier Analysis Ltd* carried out an analysis on earth samples collected from the alleged abduction site. The researchers collected fourteen samples from seven different locations, including the site where Travis was struck by the disk's burst of energy and other locations throughout the area that served as control samples. Before we go into the findings, it is important to keep in mind that at that point, the soil had endured more than forty years of weathering, including a massive forest fire in 2012. The main premise behind the analysis was that if an extraterrestrial aircraft was indeed in the area and Travis was hit by a bolt of energy, then the soil's structure would

---

[66] Clark, *High Strangeness*, 5.

have been permanently altered, and this would have been reflected in the analysis.

The analysis showed that the samples taken from the alleged abduction site had higher levels of iron with particulates compared to the other control locations. Moreover, the surface soil had higher iron levels containing particulates than the subsurface soil. One of the potential causes for this finding could be the aircraft's propulsion system, since a strong magnetic field increases the concentration of iron particulates and would have drawn them closer to the surface. The soil sample also contained higher levels of calcium, magnesium, and potassium, which further indicated a change in the soil's chemical structure. Aside from the soil samples, *Frontier Analysis Ltd.* also carried out analysis on the cored trees from the surrounding area which were first collected by Mike Rogers in 1999. The analyses on these trees were carried out in 2012, and the results showed that between 1975 to 1999, the trees experienced a rapid growth surge. Conversely, the trees that were not from the abduction site did not experience this growth. Furthermore, there was a difference in the core's circles: the circles facing the aircraft's direction were elliptical and wider than those facing the opposite direction.

Although these findings are noteworthy, it is difficult to conclusively state that they are the result of an extraterrestrial aircraft. It is also difficult to assume that these findings corroborate and support Travis's testimony. It must be mentioned once again that more than forty years had passed and the elements most certainly played a factor. For instance, the high calcium, magnesium, and potassium levels could have been caused by clay deposits. What is interesting, however, is that high iron levels are usually uncommon and are not usually caused by weathering or natural elements. Are these findings odd occurrences and anomalies, or do you believe they support Travis's narrative?

Hypotheses

Travis's story is one of the most well-known alien abduction cases, but it is also one of the most controversial ones. This leaves us with two possible hypotheses: either Travis was indeed abducted by extraterrestrials, or else this is nothing more than a well-orchestrated and elaborate hoax. In this part of the chapter we shall explore these two hypotheses and the factors which support each theory.

Hypothesis #1: An elaborate hoax

Could it be the case that Travis was kept hidden in a secret location for five days and then fabricated the alien abduction story? Unless Travis was truly abducted by an extraterrestrial entity, this is the only other plausible explanation. This hypothesis is supported by a number of factors, including: a) the lack of physical evidence, b) the lack of acetones in the urine sample, c) the fact that Travis had sound motives for fabricating this story, and d) his mother's demeanor and the fact that the Walton family were interested in the UFO phenomenon.

The first imperative factor we must consider is the lack of evidence. In our analysis we must always remain objective, and objectivity requires evidence. I am aware that many may argue that it is difficult to have evidence for close encounters, alien abductions, or the paranormal in general, but this is not the case as we have seen in previous chapters and will continue to see in subsequent chapters. For instance, many of cases explored in this book have ample evidence, and this evidence is usually a combination of physical findings at the abduction site as well as physical symptoms reported by the individual. In Travis's case there were six eyewitnesses who each described seeing a flying saucer. However, what I find odd is the fact that no markings were found at the site, even though the eyewitnesses reported a bolt of energy hitting Travis. If the bolt of energy was strong enough to send Travis a few feet off the ground, wouldn't it have left a marking on the ground?

The second factor which supports this hypothesis is the missing time period reported by Travis. When contactees report that they experienced missing time, it is usually only for a few hours and I am not aware of any other cases where the individual was reported missing for days on end. Travis, on the other hand, went missing for five entire days. Given this, if he was indeed on board an aircraft for the duration of these five days, I would presume that he would have been subjected to more medical experiments than what he recounted under hypnotic regression. Moreover, the urine analysis showed that he received some form of nutrition as there were no acetones in the urine.

The third factor is the fact that Travis had a number of motives for coming up with this narrative. The first obvious motivation is that *The National Enquirer* gave away $5,000 each year to the person with the best

UFO case. In actual fact, Travis and his colleagues won the prize that year and split the prize money between them. Aside from this, Travis earned a substantial amount of money from his memoir and movie. There is also another potential motive which could have incentivized Travis and his friends to come up with this story. In November 1971, Mike Rogers, who was Travis's boss and good friend, had a contract with the United States Forest Service to thin out the trees at Turkey Springs. The contract was a year long and was made the year before Travis's encounter. As the year was coming to an end, Rogers and his colleagues were still behind on their schedule, and they even received an eighty-four-day extension. With hundreds of acres left to cover, unless they had a solid argument, the company would lose around $2,500 for not fulfilling the contract.

This prerequisite, however, could be nullified if there were circumstances which hindered the company's work. Since inclement weather was already taken into consideration, they needed another reason. Interestingly and coincidentally, the week before Travis's disappearance, NBC-TV aired a two-hour special on Betty and Barney Hill's abduction case (this case is covered in Chapter 13). This special was well received by the public, so could it have been the case that Rogers and Walton had dawned on the perfect solution which would have saved them from paying the fine?

The fourth and final factor which supports this hypothesis is the fact that both Travis and his family were heavily interested in the UFO phenomenon. Mary's demeanor and comments throughout the investigation are also questionable and do indicate that she might have been aware of what was truly happening. Naturally, it is bizarre for a mother to tell the sheriff to call off the search as she believed her son had been abducted by aliens. Dr. Rosenbaum noted this in regard to the Walton family's interest in the UFO phenomenon:

> Everybody in the family claimed that they had seen one ... he not only comes from a "UFO-family," but from a "UFO-culture." Everybody in that area of the country sees UFOs all the time. And his brother had seen one a week or two before, and his mother had seen some. Everybody in the family had seen some and he's been preoccupied with this almost all of his life .... Then he made the comment to his mother just prior to the incident that if he was ever abducted by a UFO she was not to worry because he'd be all right.[67]

---

[67] Klass, *UFOs*, 174.

It must be mentioned that although five of the six men passed the polygraph test, Travis failed his. This result was omitted from *The National Enquirer's* feature, since it naturally contradicted the story.

Hypothesis #2: The extraterrestrial hypothesis

The first piece of evidence which supports the extraterrestrial hypothesis is the fact that there are multiple eyewitnesses. Six men, excluding Travis, described seeing a flying disk as they were driving back home. The six men also witnessed this same disk exert a bolt of energy, hitting Travis. However, an important distinction must be made between the UFO sighting and the alleged alien abduction. The men corroborated seeing the flying disk, but they naturally could not have corroborated the rest of the story since they were not present for it. They also did not witness Travis being taken on board the disk since they drove away.

Aside from the eyewitnesses, the other piece of evidence we have which supports this hypothesis is the samples which seem to indicate that the trees and soil were exposed to a strong magnetic field. The analysis carried out in 2017 indicates a change in the soil structure, and nowadays we are aware that UAP emit a strong magnetic field. However, as previously stated, the samples were subjected to more than forty years of weathering, which undoubtedly played a role in this discovery. With that being said, do these findings corroborate Travis's narrative?

▲ ▼ ▲

Conclusion

Was Travis indeed abducted by an extraterrestrial entity, or was he kept in a secret location by someone? Was this a genuine alien abduction, or just an elaborate hoax? During the writing of this chapter I admittedly found myself torn between these two hypotheses. In many UFO sightings and alien abductions, the evidence, or lack thereof, is usually conclusive and we can confidently come to an informed opinion on the matter. Travis's story, however, is not as clear-cut. As much as I wish I had the answer to what truly happened, I do not, which is what makes this case so intriguing and compelling. Travis's story has been a bone of contention for several years and will remain so for years to come.

CHAPTER 10

The visitors

Date: July–December 1985
Location: New York, United States

Whitley Strieber is the author of several fictional horror books, most notably *The Hunger* and *The Wolfen*. Later in life, Whitley became renowned for his autobiographical book, *Communion*, which details his close encounter with extraterrestrials, whom he refers to as "the visitors." Although some have dismissed his encounter as fictitious, the narrative of the abduction, description of the entities, and subsequent health deterioration make this case a noteworthy one in the study of close encounters. What follows is Whitley Strieber's life-changing encounter with the visitors, which took place in upstate New York in 1985.

> At first, I thought I was losing my mind. But I was interviewed by three psychologists and three psychiatrists, given a battery of psychological tests and a neurological examination, and found to fall within the normal range in all respects. I was also given a polygraph by an operator with thirty years' experience and I passed without qualification. I had been indifferent to the whole issue of

unidentified flying objects and extraterrestrials; I had viewed them as a false unknown, easily explainable as misperceptions or hallucinations. Now what was I to think?[68]

The encounters
July 1985

Whitley's close encounters took place in a cabin owned by his family in a remote area of upstate New York. This residence was mostly used for vacations or as a writing hub for Whitley. The first encounter occurred in the summer of 1985, and although at the time Whitley dismissed it as a mere odd occurrence, it would later be revealed that this was the first visitation he experienced, with the preeminent encounter occurring just a few months later. Although Whitley cannot remember the exact date, he recalls that the encounter took place in July in the late evening at around 23:30. While everyone was asleep, Whitley was abruptly woken up by the sound of footsteps coming from the front porch downstairs.

The cabin was located in a secluded area and was especially quiet at night, and the footsteps were loud enough to wake Whitley up. He first thought that the steps were coming from outside, but then the motion-sensitive lights were activated, indicating that someone had entered the cabin. This was naturally alarming, and Whitley immediately jolted out the bed and went downstairs, but to his surprise there was no one in sight. It is important to note that the cabin's interior is designed in such a way that every room and corner is visible, making it nearly impossible for intruders to hide. After he made sure that no one was inside, he returned to bed, assuming that the alarm system had simply malfunctioned.

4th October 1985

The incident on that July night went into the past and Whitley did not think too much of it. However, just a few months later he would experience another strange incident. It was the 4th of October 1985,

---

[68] Whitley Strieber, *Communion: A True Story* (New York: Avon, 1988), 10.

and Whitley and his wife, Ann, invited two of their close friends, Jacques and Annie, over to the cabin. After having dinner at a local restaurant, the four of them returned to the cabin and went to bed shortly thereafter. At one point during the night, a bright blue light shone from outside, illuminating the cathedral ceiling of the living room which was bright enough to wake Whitley from his sleep. From the bedroom he could see the living room, and his initial thought was that it was a car's headlights, but he then realized that it could not have projected onto the ceiling. He then presumed that it was the motion-sensitive lighting, but they did not have any bulbs installed in them at the time.

After a few seconds, the blue light started moving from a stationary position along the length of the ceiling, and the only explanation Whitley could think of was that the chimney had caught fire and sparks had fallen onto the front yard, creating an even larger fire. However, he somehow managed to go back to sleep, only to be woken up just a few moments later by a loud noise. This time, however, his wife and son had woken up as well; startled and disorientated, he perceived the room to be filled with smoke, which further confirmed his initial thought that the cabin was on fire. He dashed outside the bedroom to go near his son, where he encountered Jacques standing outside his and Annie's bedroom door. Once Whitley ensured that there weren't any fires, he returned to bed and everyone went back to sleep.

The following morning during breakfast, Annie mentioned that she and Jacques had been woken up during the night by a bright light, but she did not elaborate any further, nor did she mention hearing a loud noise. Aside from Annie, no one brought up the incident which puzzled Whitley and made him wonder whether it had all been just a dream. He was certain that he was lucid, and several months later he would learn that something sinister had actually taken place. As the days went by, Whitley began to experience inexplicable physiological symptoms; he felt lethargic most of the time and started suffering from persistent headaches. He also often recalled seeing a flashing light followed by a loud explosion. Whereas he was usually outgoing, he now felt irritable and agitated for no apparent reason. What puzzled him the most was a distinct memory he kept having which involved a massive crystal on top of the cabin's roof, emitting a bright glow. With that being said, he attributed this memory to a discombobulated dream and a few days later everything returned to normal ... until Boxing Day.

26th December 1985

The Strieber family often spent the Christmas period at the cabin, and with more than eight inches of snow, Whitley and his family spent the morning sledding and the afternoon skiing. It was indeed a peaceful and lovely day, and by 23:00 everyone had gone to bed. Similarly to what had happened in July and October, during the night Whitley was awakened by a loud noise coming from downstairs. It sounded like footsteps, but this time they were louder, as if there were several people stomping their feet.

From his bed he glanced at the alarm system and saw that it was operating, and since it had not gone off, he felt assured and went back to sleep. Just a few minutes later he was awakened once more, but this time he could see that one of the bedroom doors was closing inwards. This was not a dream—Whitley was fully conscious and lucid of his surroundings. That was the last thing Whitley was able to consciously recall. The next thing he remembered was waking up the next morning feeling uneasy and anxious. He mentioned to Ann that he distinctly remembered seeing a barn owl just outside their bedroom window.

> My mind was sharp. I was not asleep, nor in a hypnopompic state between sleep and waking. I wish to be clear that I felt, at that moment, wide awake and in full possession of all my faculties. I could easily have gotten up and read a book or listened to the radio or gone for a midnight walk in the snow.[69]

Over the next couple of days, similarly to what had happened in October, Whitley started experiencing physical ailments. He had a high temperature and felt perpetually fatigued and lethargic, despite getting more sleep than usual. He spent most of his time in bed, even when they had guests over. The back of his neck ached and so did his anal region, especially when he sat down. Aside from these physical ailments his mental health started to deteriorate as well. He felt anxious all the time and was short-tempered and irritable, even with his young son. He developed paranoia and believed he was being watched constantly. As his sleepless and restless nights persisted, his weariness grew. His condition continued to worsen, causing him to exhibit

---

[69] Strieber, *Communion*, 17–18.

depressive symptoms, but Whitley was not aware of any changes or external triggers which could have caused this. He also experienced sudden flashbacks of incongruent and strange memories which consisted of people running chaotically. None of this made any sense to him, and this sudden change worried his wife.

At this point in his life, he was oblivious to the fact that he had been abducted, but his awareness started to slowly shift when on the 3rd of January 1986, he read a story published in *Middletown New York Record* which was about several UFOs being spotted over a local prison. Prior to that moment, Whitley did not have any particular interest in UFOs, but this was a turning point in his life. After reading the article he started reading more on the phenomenon, which puzzled his wife as she thought it was completely out of character. During his reading of *Science and UFOs*, written by Jenny Randles and Peter Warrington, he learned more about what the UFO phenomenon consisted of, and he came across a case that seemed very similar to what he was going through.

In the book the authors mention Budd Hopkins, a renowned UFO researcher and expert in the field, who is best known for his research on alien abductions. Whitley looked up his phone number in the phonebook and spoke with him at length. He explained to him what he had been experiencing for the past couple of weeks, and the reality was that he felt lost and needed some guidance. No explanation made sense and he was clueless as to what had caused all of this. After speaking with Budd over the phone, they agreed to meet to explore this further, and that was the beginning of some ghastly revelations.

▲ ▼ ▲

Meeting budd hopkins
6th February 1986

His first meeting with Budd Hopkins took place on the 6th of February 1986. During the meeting, Budd asked Whitley if he had had any prior experiences with UFOs. If Whitley had been asked this question on any other day, he would have said no without a hesitation. However, he blurted out that he had, and went on to recall an incident from October where he was awakened by a loud noise and saw a bright blue light. That first meeting with Budd was nothing short of an epiphany, and afterwards he began asking his wife questions about that October night. She told him that she too had heard the noise but did not recall seeing the bright light.

Whitley asked his son about that night too and whether he had heard the loud noise or seen the bright light, and his answer took everyone by surprise. His son went on to describe a dream he had that night: after hearing the loud noise, several little people dressed as doctors surrounded him and placed him in a cot outside the cabin. Although this was terrifying, he felt safe around them and they promised they would protect him. When he asked Jacques and Annie about that night, Jacques told him that he too was woken up by a bright light. In actual fact, the light was so bright that it had lit up the entire room and at first he thought it was daytime, but the clock indicated that it was only 04:30. Annie corroborated this, and she also said that she heard footsteps coming from the room above.

> I dreamed that a bunch of little doctors took me out on the porch
> and put me on a cot. I got scared and they started saying "We won't
> hurt you" over and over in my head.[70]

The ensuing days were arduous for Whitley and Ann. Whitley started experiencing frequent nightmares and felt unsafe both at the cabin and at their home in the city, to the point that they relocated to Texas. Despite the move, he still felt scared, anxious, and unsafe. The paranoia was so intense that it started to put a strain on their marriage. That was when he decided to speak with a psychiatrist. It was evident that he was suffering from some sort of trauma and he knew that he had experienced something which he was not consciously aware of. During this period, he kept in contact with Budd Hopkins and continued to update him on what was happening. Budd provided him with solace and understanding, and as the symptoms persisted, he recommended hypnotic regression. Whitley was willing to try anything that could resolve the issue, and he agreed to give it a shot, but he wanted to choose his own hypnotherapist rather than the one Budd suggested, just to ensure there wouldn't be any biases.

---

[70] Strieber, *Communion*, 57.

Hypnotic regression

> Even after talking to Hopkins, I was by no means willing to ascribe
> my experiences to the UFO phenomenon. I wanted to be quite
> clear: I had no idea what had gone on that night.[71]

The only thing Whitley was aware of was that something traumatic
had happened, but at no point did he consider the possibility of having been abducted by an extraterrestrial entity; quite frankly, this was
the least plausible explanation for him. He made an appointment
with Dr. Donald Klein, a renowned psychiatrist who worked at the
New York State Psychiatric Institute. During the initial session, which
lasted well over three hours, Whitley gave Dr. Klein a thorough run-
down of what had happened during that past year. During the subsequent hypnotic regression sessions, Whitley would reveal that both in
October and December he was visited and captured by an extraterrestrial entity.

Revisiting the October events
Hypnosis session date: 1st March 1986

Dr. Klein guided Whitley into a hypnotic trance, and they went back to
the 4th of October 1985. Dr. Klein asked Whitley to begin recounting the
events of that day, and Whitley began by saying that they had invited
Jacques and Annie over to their cabin, and after having dinner at a local
restaurant, they returned to the cabin for the night. It was a normal,
quiet night, but at one point, a bright light woke him up from his sleep.
He opened his eyes and looked around the room, and in the corner,
just beside the door, he saw the dark silhouette of a figure. The figure
was just three foot tall, and although Whitley was fully conscious and
awake, he could not talk or move—he was glued to the bed. Back in the
clinic room, as Whitley started describing the presence of the entity, he
became distressed and started pleading to be left alone. Alas, the figure
started approaching his bed.

Now by his bedside, Whitley could see that the figure was a humanoid creature; it had distinct, slanted eyes which were both anesthetiz-
ing and horrifying at the same time. It was also wearing a hood which

---

[71] Strieber, *Communion*, 64.

covered its seemingly bald head. As Whitley had a clearer view of the being and described its features, he became increasingly anxious. Dr. Klein grounded Whitley back to the present moment and reassured him that he was safe and would not be harmed. After some moments, he guided him back to the 4th of October, where Whitley was now face-to-face with this humanoid entity.

In one of its hands, Whitley saw that the creature was holding an instrument which looked similar to a ruler. With it, he touched his forehead and at that moment, he started seeing images in his head. The first image he saw was of planet Earth going up in flames from a distance; he also heard a foreign voice in his head telling him that this was his home. The creature touched Whitley's forehead for a second time, and this time he heard a loud bang in his head, followed by an image of his son sitting in a green park. This image quickly became a tormenting one; as Whitley looked at his son from afar, he felt that the park represented death, and the idea of seeing his own son dying caused him great anguish. Whitley cried hysterically, and he heard a second voice in his head, a voice which reassured him that his son was not and would not be harmed. For the third time, the being placed the instrument against his forehead, and this time he saw the moment his father passed. Whitley was not present on the day of his father's passing, but his mother was, and she had always described it as a peaceful and painless death. Conversely, the image he was shown was antithetical to this. His father was in his bed, gasping and choking for air as his mother sat beside him, not moving a muscle as she witnessed her husband's agonizing death. As he recounted this, Whitley emerged from the hypnotic trance in a panic, mortified by what had been revealed to him.

Interestingly, the day after the hypnosis, Whitley called his mother, just like he did every other week. He did not tell her what he had been going through, and they were talking about a family friend who had recently been hospitalized. Without his prompting her, his mother started talking about his father and his passing. She described how she was sitting next to him on the couch in the living room just a few minutes before he died. Doctors had warned her that his heart would soon fail, and as she stepped out of the kitchen for a few moments, she heard him calling her name. As she returned to his side, she found him dead. It had been a painless passing indeed, just as she had been describing it all these years.

The three images Whitley was shown all elicited a similar response: fear and anxiety. The first image can be interpreted as a forewarning or a prediction of what will happen to our planet in the future. The second and third image included the death of two people whom Whitley deeply cared about and loved, his father and son. It is for this reason that I believe the purpose of this experiment was for this entity to investigate fear and anxiety in humans—perhaps they wanted to examine how we experience and process these emotions.

Revisiting the December events
Hypnosis session date: 5th March 1986

A few days after exploring the October incident, Whitley met with Dr. Klein once again, and in this session, they explored the December incident. As in the previous session, Dr. Klein first guided Whitley into a hypnotic trance, and then slowly took him back to the 26th of December 1985. Whitley first recounted how he was woken up in the middle of the night, this time by a loud noise coming from downstairs. The noise sounded like there were several people stomping their feet, moving hurriedly in the living room. From his bed he peered at the alarm system, which was still functioning, and since it had not been triggered, he went back to sleep. Just a few moments later, he was awakened once again. He felt the presence of someone or something in the room, and as he sat up, he noticed that one of the doors of the room was closing inwards. Immediately thereafter, a figure emerged, its stature like a child's, just three foot tall.

The creature stood at the entrance of the door, and as it started approaching Whitley, he felt immobilized. The creature wore a strange, smooth hat with a sharp rim that protruded four inches on one side, concealing its face. Covering its chest was a square plate with concentric circles etched on it, as well as a rectangular plate with a similar pattern beneath it that covered from the lower waist to the knees. As the being moved closer to Whitley, towards the edge of his bed, he could see its piercing black eyes and tiny slit for a mouth. It proceeded to make a gesture with its hand, and then, several other humanoid beings entered the room. These beings had similar features: they wore tight blue overalls but did not have the square and rectangular plates. They also did not wear any coverings on their heads, which exposed their hairless, smooth heads. Whitley was now surrounded by several of these humanoid beings, and he then felt completely weightless as he was being carried outside the room. Although he felt petrified, he also intuitively knew that he would not be harmed.

Whitley felt weightless as he was now being carried outside the cabin by the humanoids. As they approached a clearing in the woods, they placed him on the ground, and he realized he was completely naked. Although the temperature was sub-zero and it was snowing, he did not feel cold. He sat on the ground and from his peripheral vision he could see two figures: the first one had dark eyes and a small round mouth and for some reason he felt that it was a female. To the right side was the second figure, which was more obscure and could only be perceived when there was a flash of movement. Whitley recounted how after a few moments, he started ascending from the ground toward the sky, as if he was in an elevator, with the branches and trees moving rapidly past him. Within a few seconds he was floating atop the treetops, with the entire woods beneath him.

Throughout all of this, Whitley heard telepathic messages in his head telling him he would not be harmed, and the next thing he recalled he was sitting on a bench inside a tiny room. The room had a rounded, dome-shaped ceiling with bright fluorescent lights. He could smell a pungent odor and as he sat on the bench with his back to the wall, he observed several of the humanoids moving around rapidly. One of them approached him; it had an enlarged head with bulging, dark eyes. Its skin looked as though it was made of leather. The creature communicated telepathically with Whitley, telling him that they would now be carrying out some medical experiments. Whitley objected to this, claiming that they had no right to do this, but alas, the creature dismissed his protest. He was then led into one of the rooms which had two creatures, one of which was holding a rectangular box, and inside was a thin needle mounted on a black surface.

Whitley was told that this needle would be inserted into his brain and this horrified him; he started shouting in a panic, but after hearing a loud bang, everything went black. Once he regained consciousness, he found himself in a different room which had a table in its center and three benches. Inside the room were several of these creatures; one of them approached Whitley with an enormous, triangular gray instrument with several wires attached to its end. He was told that the instrument would be inserted into his rectum so that they could collect a fecal sample. The procedure was quick and painless, and after this, his mouth was inspected. This was followed by a small incision on one of his fingers. This was the last medical procedure Whitley recalled. Following this, he found himself sitting on the couch of his living room, completely naked and oblivious to what had happened. He climbed the stairs to their bedroom, changed into his pajamas, and fell asleep, unaware that his life was about to change forever.

> I went sailing right back into my living room in no more than a minute. I had no memory of where I had just come from. I sat on the couch.[72]

▲ ▼ ▲

Ann's hypnosis

Despite these revelations, Whitley was still hesitant about accepting this new reality. As he disclosed to Ann what he had uncovered through hypnosis, they agreed that it would be beneficial and insightful if she also underwent hypnotic regression as this would provide them with her perspective of that night. She met with Dr. Robert Naiman, and in the first sessions they went over the October incident. Similarly to Whitley, Ann described how they had Jacques and Annie over at the cabin, and after a pleasant dinner they returned to the cabin for the night.

Ann went on to say that at one point during the night, Whitley woke her up in a panic, telling her that the roof was on fire. A few moments later she heard a loud noise followed by her son screaming. The scream was heartbreaking to hear, and as much as she wanted to go comfort her son and find out what had happened to him, she explained how she felt she wasn't supposed to leave the room. The feeling was hard to explain, and as Dr. Naiman probed further, Ann described how she felt lonely and uneasy, and something was telling her not to turn the light on as she was not supposed to see what was happening. Dr. Naiman asked her who she was referring to, but Ann did not have an answer; she simply said that there was another woman who was comforting her child. The only other woman in the cabin was Annie, but she did not leave her bedroom that night.

In the following sessions, Ann and Dr. Naiman explored the December incident, which started off by Ann being woken up by Whitley. This time he told her that he had seen a bright crystal in the sky and a barn owl looking through their bedroom window. She too felt the presence

---

[72] Strieber, *Communion*, 128.

of a figure by her side, and when she opened her eyes, she saw a white figure thumping her in the stomach. The jab was excruciatingly painful, and at that instant she heard her son shouting. With that being said, she felt immobilized—she couldn't get up or do anything. When she asked her son why he had screamed the night before, he explained that he had had a nightmare involving a terrifying white figure.

The presence of a white figure in the room was a recurrent nightmare for their son, and he spoke about this with his babysitter on numerous occasions. Furthermore, several months later at school, he was assigned to write about a dream for a project, and he wrote a story in which he was captured from his bed and placed in a cot outside the cabin. Surrounding him were several doctors with large, dark eyes. The doctors first examined his nose and then his arm with a device which emitted an orange light that allowed them to see through the skin. Throughout his upbringing, Whitley and Ann did not disclose to him what his father had gone through; they wanted him to explore it himself if he felt inclined to do so when he got older.

▲ ▼ ▲

Hypotheses

Hypothesis #1: A brain condition

Whitley was never interested in the UFO phenomenon or the paranormal and he believed there was a rational explanation for the symptoms he was experiencing. Over the years he has undergone several tests and examinations, and each test showed that he was not suffering from any organic problems in the brain. It was only after every possible hypothesis was ruled out that he believed this was an otherworldly encounter.

In December 1986, Whitley underwent an EEG to explore whether he suffered from temporal lobe epilepsy, which causes vivid hallucinations. One of the symptoms of temporal lobe epilepsy is spike charges in the temporal lobe, especially during sleep. However, the test ruled this out and the doctors concluded that "there were no persistent asymmetries, focal abnormalities or epileptiform discharges." In March 1988, Whitley underwent an MRI to rule out any other brain abnormalities. The scan did reveal previously unknown bright objects in the brain, and when these objects are large enough, they may indicate muscular dystrophy. With that being said, the finding was "medically insignificant" and the doctor ruled out any other brain anomalies.

In February 1986, two months after the December incident, Whitley underwent a psychological test which revealed that he was under "a good deal of stress." The psychologists observed how this stress manifested itself physically, and many of the physical ailments he suffered were a projection of the inner turmoil he was experiencing. Furthermore, the psychologist observed how Whitley "appeared to be very frightened and powerless." Several years later, Whitley was still suffering psychologically as a result of the encounter, and this was reflected in the psychological test that was administered fifteen years later, in January 1999. Throughout the years, Whitley has also undergone several polygraph tests, with the administrator reaching the same conclusion in each test: that Whitley was telling the truth.

All of these tests together conclude with two findings: a) the encounter was not a result of any brain abnormalities or psychological disorders, and b) Whitley believed that what he had recounted had actually occurred. Although these two findings are significant, they do not give us a conclusive answer as to what truly happened. This leaves us with two other possible hypotheses: either Whitley is telling the truth and was indeed abducted by an extraterrestrial entity, or the entire story is a hoax.

Hypothesis #2: The extraterrestrial hypothesis

Before we explore this hypothesis, it is important to remember that it is difficult to conclusively prove that an alien abduction did take place. We usually reach this conclusion after ruling out every other possibility and if the case has an overwhelming amount of evidence. In this case, we must first acknowledge Whitley's narrative and the fact that it is deeply engrossing and informative. The extraterrestrial hypothesis is supported by the immediate and intermediate aftereffects experienced; however, aside from this, there aren't any other pieces of evidence.

Hypothesis #3: A hoax

The last hypothesis we shall explore is the possibility of this case being a hoax. One of the factors which we must acknowledge and remain mindful of is the fact that Whitley is an exceptional fictional writer. He has had numerous books on the best-seller list, and it is undeniable that he knows how to write a compelling and impressive story. Keeping this in mind, is it possible that this encounter was just another horror story, a plot for a new book? His autobiographical book, which details his encounter, remained a best-seller for six months, and whether the details in the book are true or not, he certainly made a profit from it. With that being said, as I have stated previously in this book, just because a profit was made from the encounter does not conclusively determine that the case is a hoax.

▲ ▼ ▲

Exclusive interview with Whitley Strieber

In 2019, I had the privilege of speaking with Whitley himself and to ask him some questions related to his encounter.

When was the first time you considered that you might have been abducted by visitors?

I ran out of other explanations. When my doctor told me that I had physical injuries, I knew that something had happened. After looking at all the effects that I had, there was only one explanation. I do not know who did this. I did not know why they had, nor do I know now. I am not sure if what I experienced were aliens. All I do know is that these beings are extremely advanced.

Could you explain what happened during one of the abductions?

There was only one real abduction. I had woken up in some place that I did not know of, with no explanation as to how I had gotten there. During this abduction, medical experiments were carried out for some reason that I do not know of to this day.

What do you think these visitors wanted from you?

I am still in communication with them and I am still working on the question of what they want. It is a large existential question, ultimately larger than my own life. However, I will keep addressing this in as many ways as I possibly can, as I have been doing for the past thirty years.

Do you see a difference between the person you were before the abduction and the person after?

I was happy and innocent. That has changed.

Do you think that these visitors had malicious intentions?

I do not personally think that this question can be answered in a straight-forward way. We are very complex, and you cannot say an individual is either all good or all bad. Real people do not divide into groups that way. The visitors, who are extremely more complex than us do not divide in that way either.

What was your reaction after finding out that you had been abducted after the hypnosis sessions?

I was confused and appalled by the hypnosis session if I am being honest. It was during the session that for the first time, I perceived these other beings in terms of personalities with a sense of individuation about them.

Why do you think extraterrestrials are so interested in Earth and humanity?

My impression is that they are concerned about whether or not we are going to go extinct. I personally think that they would rather we not do that.

Do you think that consciousness and spirituality are one of the reasons why humans are abducted by these visitors? Or is their interest solely in the human anatomy?

This is about the soul. What it is, what it means and why we are soul blind and how to wake us up. I believe that this is initiatory on a massive scale. The physical part is secondary. The primary reason behind the abduction cases is the human psyche.

Conclusion

The detailed narrative makes Whitley's encounter one of the most famous alien abduction cases to date. One of the things which stuck with me the most was how deeply it affected Whitley and his family. In fact, he summed up the aftermath in a single profound sentence: "I was happy and innocent. That has changed." Many have been quick to dismiss the case as a hoax, but I believe that this case is an imperative one in the study of alien abductions as there is a lot to be learned from it. That being said, different people will have different perspectives on the case's veracity, and due to the limited evidence we have, it all comes down to beliefs. Alien abductions, as Whitley correctly stated, are as much about the soul as they are about human anatomy, and it is now time to investigate why so many of us have become "soul blind" and to investigate what it means to be human. I would like to close this chapter with Whitley's answer to the last question:

"This is about the soul. What it is, what it means and why we are soul blind and how to wake us up. I believe that this is initiatory on a massive scale. The physical part is secondary. The primary reason behind the abduction cases is the human psyche."

CHAPTER 11

The Pascagoula abduction

Date: 11th October 1974
Location: Mississippi, United States

Charlie Hickson was a forty-two-year-old Korean war veteran who worked at the dockyard as a shipfitter in Pascagoula. Some years prior to 1973, he had arranged for Calvin Parker, his friend's son, to join the shipyard as well. Calvin and Charlie's friendship dated back several years; Calvin often recalled going on fishing trips with his father and Charlie as a child, and now the two upheld the tradition by going on short fishing trips by the Pascagoula River after their workday at the shipyard. On a typical day, they finished work at around 17:00 and would then go home, pack their fishing equipment and drive down highway 90 towards the river where they would spend some hours fishing. The 11th of October 1973, however, was a day unlike any other. This is the Pascagoula encounter—the fascinating story of Calvin and Charlie, and one of the most credible alien abduction cases of all time.

The encounter
11th October 1973

The day went in a seemingly routine fashion. By 17:00 Calvin and Charlie left the shipyard and drove towards the Pascagoula River where they planned on spending some time unwinding and fishing. During their drive there Charlie told Calvin that he had discovered a new spot which was ostensibly ideal since many ships unloaded grains in the vicinity, and some would spill into the river, attracting a lot of fish. It must have been around 18:00 when they arrived at the river; prior to going to the new location Charlie had discovered, they went over to their usual spot, the East River. There, they unloaded their fishing equipment and sat on some old timber as they waited patiently for the bait to attract the fish. Several minutes passed by and they still had not caught any fish, but Charlie was a stubborn and determined man and did not want to walk away empty-handed, so he insisted on staying there just a little while longer.

Sitting by the river was exactly what the two men needed after a day of work. It was peaceful and rejuvenating, but the tranquil mood was shortly interrupted by a startling zipping noise, which first started off at a low frequency and then got progressively louder. Calvin and Charlie looked around to identify the source, but they were unable to locate where it was coming from. After a few seconds, a pulsating blue light appeared. They first thought it was the siren of a police car, perhaps to tell them to leave the area, but there were no cars in sight. Just as Calvin turned, he saw an oddly shaped aircraft hovering just two feet off the ground and a few feet away from them. The aircraft was oval-shaped, just like a rugby ball, and it was around eight feet high with a dome structure on top. The blue light it was emitting was blinding, and then a hatch in the center of the aircraft opened, letting out a piercing white light from the inside. Calvin and Charlie just stared at each other, stunned by what was ahead of them and unaware of what was about to unfold. As the entrance to the aircraft opened, the dark silhouettes of three creatures emerged, blocking the light. This was the beginning of a transformative experience for Calvin and Charlie.

The three creatures stood at around five foot tall and had grey colored skin. Their bodies were covered in wrinkles to the point that they couldn't make out any facial features, except for the nose and ears which were cone-shaped and came to a point. Their heads came directly to their shoulders as they lacked a neck, and they had long limbs with mitten-like hands and pincers for fingers. Their feet were adjoined together and were elevated off the ground. In fact, they did not walk, but hovered towards Calvin and Charlie's position. This was a ghastly sight, and as the three creatures approached the pair, they felt immobilized and glued to the ground, unable to move. It was something out of a horror film, but even though they knew the ending was not going to be a good one, they had to sit through it and endure the experience nonetheless.

Charlie's encounter

As the three creatures reached their position, two of them grabbed Charlie by the arm, one on each of his sides, while the third one went over to Calvin. He felt an instant sharp pain as the pincer-like appendages touched his body. Charlie was rendered immobile, and from his peripheral vision he could see that the third creature had grabbed Calvin, who had now fainted and gone limp. He wanted to shout at Calvin, to tell him to fight back, but he couldn't—something was controlling his body. The two creatures glided towards the aircraft, escorting Charlie inside and they entered the first room, which was bare and cold.

The room was illuminated by a blinding white light and the creatures proceeded to place Charlie against a wall and then exited the room. There, a device which resembled a human eye emerged from the wall and started scanning his body, from his head down to his legs. Once the device circled his body, it retracted back into the wall and the two creatures entered the room once more. Charlie was a war veteran who was unfazed by many things, but this encounter had surpassed anything he had witnessed in his life. He was desperate for this encounter to come to an end, but alas he had to endure it all.

> Why in hell don't they just stop me from breathing and let my life end here?[73]

As the two grim creatures re-entered the room, they approached Charlie and grabbed him by the shoulders. They proceeded to escort

---

[73] Calvin Parker, *Pascagoula—The Closest Encounter: My Story* (West Yorkshire, UK: Flying Disk Press, 2018), 51.

him outside the aircraft, placing him exactly where they had captured him. There he saw Calvin on the ground, with his limbs outstretched, shell-shocked and in a complete daze. The aircraft's entrance closed, and the pulsating blue light and zipping noise returned as the aircraft lifted from the ground. The aircraft shot up toward the sky, disappearing in an instant. At that moment, despite the harrowing experience he had gone through, a foreign thought entered his mind, telling him that "they" did not have malicious intentions and had not intended to cause him any harm.

Calvin's encounter

As the third creature grabbed Calvin by the arm, he felt a sharp pain as its pincer-like appendages pierced his body, and the next day he discovered a corresponding puncture mark. Ahead of him he could see Charlie being escorted by the two creatures towards the oval-shaped aircraft, and upon their entering, Charlie was taken to the first room while Calvin was taken into a different one. The room felt cold and was lit up by a blinding white light. It was also empty, except for an examination table in the center on which he was lying. The creature left the room and he began hearing a clicking noise. Above him, he noticed a square device the size of a deck of cards that scanned and rotated four times around his body before another creature entered the room.

This being appeared different to the rest: it looked less mechanical and more human-like; it had a smaller frame and a thinner face with distinct brown eyes. Calvin was aware that he could have easily overpowered him, but simultaneously, another thought entered his mind, telling him that he would not be harmed. At that moment, a second device emerged from the wall and scanned his body once more. After this, the larger, eerie being that had captured him re-entered the room and escorted him outside the aircraft. He was placed on the ground, and after a few seconds, Charlie appeared. The entrance to the aircraft then closed, and the blue light and zipping noise returned. In an instant, the oval-shaped aircraft took off towards the sky.

▲ ▼ ▲

Calvin and Charlie sat on the ground for some minutes as they tried to regain their composure. They were left speechless and quite frankly had no idea what they had just experienced. While they wished this was nothing more than a nightmare, they knew that it had truly happened. They talked with one another and discussed what had happened inside, and it seemed that they were both subjected to similar experiments. However, although they both knew that what they had just experienced did really happen, they were confident no one else would see it that way. How would they even begin to explain it? They were both shaken up, but Calvin appeared to be more distraught and traumatized, and having to recount the incident over and over would only traumatize him further. They deliberated for several minutes and after going back and forth several times, they agreed they would keep the entire incident to themselves. And so, they gathered their equipment and started walking back towards their car.

As they reached the vehicle, they saw that the window on the passenger's side was completely shattered but still in place, however, once they opened the door, it collapsed to the ground. Moreover, the engine stalled for several minutes before they were able to start it back up. During their drive back home, they discussed the encounter further, and the reality was that they were terrified these beings would return and capture them once again. It was this fear that pushed Calvin and Charlie to make a formal police report, and this marked the beginning of a daunting and unnerving period in their lives.

▲ ▼ ▲

The Investigation
11th October 1973

Calvin and Charlie stopped the car at the nearest payphone, where they phoned Keesler Air Force Base. They described their encounter to the operator, who informed them that they did not handle such reports and recommended they speak with their local sheriff. They phoned the sheriff's office and spoke with Sheriff Fred Diamond, who asked the men to go down by the station so that they could file a formal report and have a proper conversation on what had happened. Prior to arriving at the station, Calvin was still hesitant about talking about their experience, and while Charlie was able to contain his emotions and shock, Calvin was visibly distressed and shaken up. To protect Calvin, they both agreed that they would inform the sheriff that Calvin had fainted and had no recollection of what had occurred. This would allow Charlie to do the majority of the talking and relieve Calvin from having to relive his experience once again.

At the sheriff's office they recounted the story, starting from their workday at the shipyard to what happened at the river. Charlie went into great detail about the oval-shaped aircraft and the creatures, and they stayed inside the sheriff's office for several hours. Naturally, the sheriff was skeptical of such a story and suspected that they were making it all up, but he also knew that if this was the case, they were not going to simply admit to it. To try to catch them in the lie, the sheriff planted a tape recorder in the desk drawer without informing them and left the office, leaving Charlie and Calvin alone. As they were alone, he was expecting them to discuss how they were going to maintain the lie between themselves, and the truth would then be revealed. And the truth was revealed indeed. As the sheriff left the office, Calvin and Charlie continued to talk about what they had experienced. Their story remained consistent, and it was clear that they were both shaken by what they had gone through.

This secret tape was a pivotal point in the investigation as it proved to the sheriff that the pair were indeed telling the truth. This secret tape has also made this encounter one of the most credible and reputable accounts in the study of the alien abductions. What follows is the transcript of their conversation:

Calvin   I can't take much more of that. I got to get home and get to bed or get some nerve pills or see the doctor or something. I can't stand it. I'm about to go half crazy.

Charlie   I tell you, when we're through, I'll get you something to settle you down so you can get some damn sleep.

Calvin   I can't sleep yet like it is. I'm just damn near crazy.

Charlie   Well, Calvin, when they brought you out—when they brought me out of that thing, goddamn it I like to never in hell got you straightened out.

Calvin   My damn arms, my arms, I remember they just froze up and I couldn't move. Just like I stepped on a damn rattlesnake. I passed out. I expect I never passed out in my whole life.

Charlie   I've never seen nothin' like that before in my life. You can't make people believe in that though. I don't give a shit whether they believe it or not, 'cause I know.

Charlie   They'd better wake up and start believing.
Calvin   You're damn right.
Charlie   They'd better wake up and start believing.
Calvin   You're damn right.
Charlie   They'd better wake up and start believing.
Calvin   'Cause I seen 'em. I can't figure out the damn thing—did
          you see how that door come right open in front of us all of a
          sudden?
Charlie   Yeah, I don't know how it opened, son. I don't know
Calvin   I didn't see no swing or …
Charlie   I don't know how it opened—I don't know how it opened I
          didn't see it open. All I seen was this here "zip." Have you
          ever seen something.
Calvin   Then looked around—them damn blue lights and them sons-
          a-bitches was just—just like they come out.
Charlie   I know. You can't believe it. You can't make people believe it.
Calvin   I paralyzed right then. I couldn't move.
Charlie   They won't believe it. They gonna believe it one of these days.
          Might be too late. I knew all along they were people from
          other worlds up there. I knew all along. I never thought it
          would happen to me.
Calvin   You know yourself I don't drink.
Charlie   I know, I know that.
Calvin   We're going to be accused of being a damn dope-head and
          everything else—'cause I know I ain't!
Charlie   Any very little I drink—and I drank some a while ago when I
          got out of the damn thing, to settle my nerves. And I'll prob-
          ably take me a couple of drinks when I get to the house and
          make me sleep.
Calvin   I'll tell you something, if I thought it would help my nerves
          I'd go drink something right now.
Charlie   When I get to the house, I'm gonna get me another drink,
          make me sleep. Look, what we sittin' around for. I gotta go
          tell Blanche … why did they say we had to wait?
Calvin   Uh—I got to go to the house. I am done sitting here getting so
          damn sick right now, I ain't shittin' ya. I got to go to the house.
Charlie   Wait a minute; let me go talk to 'em.[74]

---

[74] Parker, *Pascagoula—The Closest Encounter*, 73–84.

It was around 23:00 by the time they finished talking with the sheriff, and the drive back home was deafeningly quiet. They both slept very little that night, and the next morning they awoke and returned to work, expecting and hoping that things would be the same as they were the day before, but this was not to be the case. Upon their arrival at the shipyard, their colleagues immediately noticed that something was wrong with Calvin, who still could not conceal the shock. Furthermore, a few hours into the day, Charlie received a phone call from a news reporter in Jackson, Mississippi, who began questioning him about their encounter at the river the day before. This phone call angered Charlie as he expected the sheriff to keep the details confidential. He immediately called Sheriff Diamond's office and expressed his outrage and dismay, and while the sheriff reassured Charlie that it wasn't him who had spoken to the press, he was correct in stating that a story like this would have reached the public sooner rather than later.

From there on, the number of phone calls increased as the day went by; they received phone calls from all around the country, and they all asked the same questions pertaining to the day before. It was also evident that they could not hide this story from their colleagues any longer, so they confided in their good friend Jim Flying. As they spoke to Jim and described their experience, he made a quick sketch of the aliens' appearance based on their description. The phone calls did not cease, to the point that the manager of the shipyard, Oliver Bryant, asked to speak with Calvin and Charlie in his office. Johnny Walker, the owner of the shipyard, also joined them. The men recounted their experience once more, and Bryant and Walker suggested they bring in a legal team, at the very least for advice, so they contacted local attorney Joe Colingo. The first thing Colingo suggested was that they undergo a polygraph test to immediately prove that they were being truthful and sincere.

Together with their lawyer, they drove down to the sheriff's office, which at this point was swarming with news reporters. Charlie also requested to be tested for radiation exposure, but Sheriff Diamond told them that they lacked the necessary equipment and thus directed them to Keesler Air Force base. At the Air Force base they were immediately tested and it was confirmed that they had not been exposed to radiation. However, prior to their departure they were approached by an intelligence officer who asked to speak with them in his office. As they went over their story again, the officer informed them that the base had received a number of phone calls from people in the area describing unusual aircraft and bright lights in the sky on the day of their encounter, and the days leading up to it. At that moment they felt relieved; even though they were unaware of what had happened or who those beings were—at least their story was being taken seriously.

The corroborating reports

The corroborating reports are an integral part of the story as they add credibility to the case. The first report we shall explore was made on the same day as Calvin and Charlie's encounter and was made late in the evening by Larry Booth, a service station operator. It was around 21:00 and Larry was at his residence; as he was closing his windows and locking his doors, a bright light coming from outside caught his eyes. As he peered outside the windows he saw a disk-shaped aircraft traveling at a low altitude, completely silently. Larry then reported that the aircraft made a rapid acceleration and disappeared in an instant. The second report was made by Raymond Broadus, a probation officer. At some point during the night Raymond observed an oblong shaped object in the sky hovering motionlessly and silently. He initially thought it was a helicopter, but there were no visible rotors and it moved completely silently. It hovered for several minutes before it disappeared.

A day before Charlie and Calvin's encounter, a similar report was made by a highly credible witness, Robert Lonardo in Orleans Parish, Louisiana. A police lieutenant, Lonardo was on duty when he started receiving several phone calls from individuals describing the same peculiarly shaped aircraft and bright lights in the sky. Lieutenant Lonardo went to Jimmy Fisher's residence, one of the individuals who made the report, and just outside his house he saw a silver, disk-shaped aircraft hovering in the sky, emitting a very distinct and strange noise. Lonardo had a tape recorder in his vehicle and he managed to record it. The sound was of a very high-pitched frequency which came to an abrupt stop. Simultaneously, the aircraft shot up toward the sky and disappeared. In the subsequent days, several more reports of a similar nature were made.

▲ ▼ ▲

The press release

In the days following their encounter, the news spread all over the country and many news media outlets were covering the otherworldly encounter at the Pascagoula river. Two of the people who contacted Calvin and Charlie were Dr. J. Allen Hynek, an astronomer and one of the advisors for Project Blue Book, and Dr. James Harder. The day following the encounter, on the 12th of October, Hynek and Harder went to Pascagoula to speak with the men themselves, and after talking with them at length, they recommended they undergo hypnotic regression.

They agreed, and Charlie was the first to undergo hypnosis. As Dr. Harder guided him into a calm, hypnotic state, they went back to the previous day. Charlie recalled arriving at the East River with Calvin and seeing the oval-shaped aircraft soon after. He proceeded to recount the events which unfolded, but he grew agitated and distressed, to the point that Dr. Harder brought him back to the present moment and ended the session. After Charlie it was Calvin's turn. Similarly, however, he was too distressed and overwhelmed, and thus Dr. Harder ended the session shortly into it.

> I was back there with the craft landing and those things coming out. I believe now hypnotism could shed a lot more light, but two days after! My god, I couldn't stand it. I'm human too; I can only take so much.[75]

The fear and terror in the men's voices was testament to how horrifying the ordeal had been for them. Later on in the day, Hynek and Harder delivered a news conference pertaining to the Pascagoula encounter.

> Hynek: There's simply no question in my mind that these men have had a very real, frightening experience, the physical nature of which I am not certain about—and I don't think we have any answers to that. But I think we should very definitely point out that under no circumstances should these men be ridiculed. They are absolutely honest. They have had a fantastic experience and also I believe, it should be taken in context with experiences that others have had elsewhere in this country and in the world.

---

[75] Parker, *Pascagoula – The Closest Encounter*, 60.

Harder: The many reports made over the past twenty, thirty years point to an objective reality that is not terrestrial. When you've eliminated all the probable explanations, and you still have something that you know is real, you're left with the less probable explanations, and I've been left with the conclusion—that we're dealing with an extraterrestrial phenomenon. I can say so beyond any reasonable doubt.

Question: Where do you think the craft came from?

Harder: Where they're from or why they're here is a matter for speculation.

Question: Then you think what Hickson and Parker are saying is what happened?

Harder: The experience that they underwent was indeed a real one. A very strong feeling of terror is practically impossible to fake under hypnosis.

Question: Do UFOs pose any threat? Do we have reason to fear them?

Harder: If you pick up a mouse in a laboratory situation, it's very frightening to the mouse. But it doesn't mean that you mean the mouse any harm.[76]

The aftermath

The ensuing months were troublesome and challenging for Charlie and Calvin. The media continued to cover their encounter extensively, and they were even invited to appear on the *Dick Cavett Show*. In the background, however, Calvin's mental health continued to deteriorate drastically, to the point that he suffered a complete nervous breakdown and had to hospitalized. He left Pascagoula and avoided any form of attention from the press. Being disconnected from the scene served him well, and even after his recovery he decided against returning to Pascagoula. He wanted a fresh start and Calvin only talked about his experience publicly many decades later in an autobiographical memoir. Charlie, on the other hand, went on to appear on the *Dick Cavett Show* where

---

[76] Ralph Blum and Judy Blum, *Beyond Earth: Man's Contact with UFOs* (New York: Bantam Books, 1974), 24–25.

he recounted his experience in front of more than two million viewers worldwide. He later made several other media appearances and was subjected to polygraph tests on numerous occasions, with each test confirming that he was telling the truth.

> This is to certify that I, Scott Glasgow, polygraph operator for Pendleton Detective Agency of New Orleans, Louisiana, at the request of Joe Colingo, attorney at law in Pascagoula, Mississippi, and the Jackson County sheriff's Office, did, on October 30, 1973, conduct a polygraph examination of Charles Hickson regarding the truthfulness of his statements that he saw a spaceship, three space creatures, and was taken into the spaceship on October 11, 1973. It is my opinion that Charles Hickson told the truth when he stated (1) that he believed he saw a spaceship, (2) that he was taken into the spaceship, (3) that he believed he saw three space creatures.[77]

Hypotheses

Hypothesis #1: A hypnagogic state

The first theory we shall explore is that the two men were in a hypnagogic state at the time of the encounter, which is the transitional state between wakefulness and sleep, where visual and audible hallucinations are commonly experienced. Charlie and Calvin both reported feeling a floating sensation as they were led into the disk, and this floating sensation is common in a hypnagogic state. So, could this be all there is to the story? Although this theory cannot be completely dismissed, it is highly unlikely that both men entered this state at the same time and had similar experiences. The corroborating sightings also lend credence to Charlie and Calvin's story.

Hypothesis #2: A hoax

The second hypothesis is the possibility of this case being a hoax. This theory can be debunked by a number of factors. To begin with, it would be contradictory to state that Charlie and Calvin came up with a hoax

---

[77] Blum & Blum, *Beyond Earth*, 198.

for fame and money, only for Calvin to avoid it at all costs due to the psychological distress he was experiencing. Second, the corroborating UFO sightings do seem to indicate that the area was a hotspot for UFO sightings. Lastly, if the pair had fabricated the entire story, what would have been their motive? They did gain attention and did appear on famous television shows, but at no point did they continually seek this attention. Even after their encounter, they continued to live simple and modest lifestyles.

Hypothesis #3: The extraterrestrial hypothesis

The final hypothesis we shall explore is the extraterrestrial hypothesis, and there are several factors that support this theory and add credibility to the case. The first, and perhaps most important factor to mention is the secret tape that Sheriff Diamond planted in his office. This tape proved to the sheriff that Charlie and Calvin were telling the truth and that the men's story was genuine. If they had been lying, they would have been bound to discuss it when they were left alone in his office.

The second critical factor is the corroborating reports made the day before their encounter, on the day of the encounter, and on subsequent days. Throughout this period, multiple reports of a similar nature were made, all describing a disk-shaped, unconventional aircraft in the sky hovering for some time before making a rapid acceleration and disappearing out of sight. Although we do not know whether these reports were directly linked to Charlie and Calvin's encounter, it is apparent that the area surrounding the Pascagoula river was a hotspot for UAPs at this time. The third and final factor we shall examine is the immediate and intermediate aftereffects, especially those reported by Calvin. Following the incident, Calvin experienced a drastic deterioration in his mental health, to the point that he had to be hospitalized and leave Pascagoula.

▲ ▼ ▲

Conclusion

After reading the narrative and the evidence, it is now up to you, the reader, to form your own informed opinion about what happened that day. Was this a genuine close encounter of the fourth kind, or just a hypnagogic hallucination? Were Calvin and Charlie truly abducted by the heinous creatures they described, or was it all a figment of their imagination? Over five decades have now passed since Calvin and Charlie's close encounter at the Pascagoula river, and to this day, this case remains one of the most fascinating and compelling cases in the study of close encounters.

CHAPTER 12

The Kentucky abductions

Date: 6th January 1976
Location: Kentucky, United States

The Kentucky abductions are without a doubt one of the most compelling and convincing cases in the study of alien abductions, and the
overwhelming amount of indisputable evidence demonstrates why.
The following encounter took place on the 6th of January 1976, the day
of Mona Stafford's birthday, which she was celebrating at a local restaurant with two of her good friends, Louise Smith and Elaine Thomas.
What started off as a pleasant evening between three good friends
turned into an unfathomable and traumatic encounter that would forever change the lives of these three women. This is the story of Mona,
Louise, and Elaine.

The Encounter
6th January 1976

The time was around 23:15 when Mona, Louise, and Elaine finished their meal and started their drive back home along route 78. Louise was driving, with Mona in the passenger seat and Elaine in the back. The drive was a smooth and pleasant one with very little traffic on the road; however, things took a turn shortly into the drive when Mona noticed a bright red light in the sky; it was so bright that she pointed it out to Louise and Elaine and they initially thought it was either an aircraft about to make a crash landing or a bright meteorite. The light kept moving across the sky, but after a few seconds, the women's theories on what it could have been were quickly disproved as it began to move erratically, making precise, sharp, and intentional maneuvers. It started moving from side to side and they judged its size to be "bigger than two houses."[78]

After a few moments it started to dawn on the women that they were witnessing something unconventional, for no aircraft they were aware of could perform such unimaginable maneuvers. The light swiftly moved from side to side and made rapid accelerations with abrupt turns and halts. It was simply limitless and defied every law of physics and aerodynamics. Their fascination quickly turned into concern as they noticed that the light was progressively getting closer to the vehicle. Once it was close enough for them to discern its characteristics, the concern turned into fear; it was "enormous, metallic and disk-shaped with a dome on top with a ring of red lights at the center and a single yellow light near the under-belly."[79] What made the sight even eerier was the fact that this aircraft was inching closer to the vehicle, and shortly thereafter, Louise abruptly lost control over the car.

At the front, Louise shouted in a panic as she tried to regain control over the car—she took her foot completely off the accelerator and slammed on the breaks, but somehow the car maintained its velocity and momentum. The ignition light turned on, indicating that the engine was stalling, and yet the car was still speeding at 85 miles per hour! Mona grabbed the steering wheel herself to assist Louise, but to no avail.

[78] Leonard Stringfield, "The Stanford, Kentucky Abduction", *The MUFON UFO Journal*, 110 (1977).
[79] Ibid.

In future interviews Louise emphasized how her foot was completely off the pedal but alas the car continued to speed. There was complete chaos, and in addition to this, the disk-shaped aircraft was now hovering in close proximity. They had no idea what the disk was, but whoever was piloting it was evidently aware of their position, as it was maneuvering in relation to the car.

From the rearview mirror, Louise observed how the disk was now tailing their car and saw it perform a complete flip on its end, exposing its underside. The disk continued to maneuver and then swiftly glided towards the driver's side, emitting a bluish-white light that illuminated the road ahead and the car's interior. At that moment, Mona, Louise, and Elaine noticed that something similar to fog filled the interior of the car, causing an intense burning sensation all over their bodies. Moreover, the light was so intense that it impaired their vision, and the next thing they knew, the car was backed up against the bordering wall of a nearby farm. As they opened their eyes, they realized that an hour and twenty minutes had gone by and they were on the outskirts of Hustonville, eight miles away from where they had last recalled being.

By the time they arrived at Louise's trailer in Liberty it was 01:20 and approximately two hours had passed since they had left the restaurant. Their bodies were covered in burn marks, and they were completely horrified; there were no words to describe what they had just experienced. They were also unaware of what to do next, so they sought assistance from Louise's neighbor, Lowell Lee. They recounted the story to Lowell, and he could see the burn marks on their bodies and their irritated eyes. In addition, each of them discovered a red mark on the back of their necks, and while Louise was washing her face in the bathroom, she noticed that the minute hand on her watch was moving as fast as the second hand. They were all agitated and shaken up, so they called the police station to file a report, but their phone call was quickly dismissed. They then called the local Navy station but after recounting their experience, they were told there wasn't much they could do to assist. After their phone calls were ignored, they realized they would be mocked if they spoke to anyone about it, so they collectively agreed to try move on and forget the incident.

Unfortunately, this was just the beginning of what can only be described as a desolate period in their lives; the burn marks and irritation did not subside, and in the coming days they started receiving phone calls from news reporters inquiring about the phone call they had made to the Navy the night of the incident. It was only a matter of time before a story like this spread like wildfire, and within a few days, news stations all over Kentucky began covering their case.

The aftermath

> When I went into the bathroom, I burnt just like I was scalding myself from the heat (Louise Smith).[80]

From the early hours of the 7th of January onwards, the burning sensation the three women experienced became more intense and persistent as the hours passed. The following day, they visited a doctor who suspected radiation exposure. More days went by and their condition did not improve; conversely, it continued to deteriorate. Over the span of a few days, Mona, Elaine, and Louise all experienced similar symptoms, most notably an insatiable thirst, rapid weight loss, and insomnia. Aside from the physical symptoms, they felt constantly agitated and overwhelmed, and their friends observed how they began chain smoking.

Interestingly enough, they also observed mechanical anomalies following their incident. For instance, Louise's Chevy Nova, the same vehicle they were in that night, started experiencing electrical failures. The signal lights would unexpectedly stop working and as a consequence she was pulled over by the patrol police on numerous occasions. Moreover, the minute hand on her wrist watch continued to move as quickly as the second hand, and this anomaly was also noticed in her bedroom alarm clock.

Perhaps the most bizarre of incidents was the imminent death of Louise's pet parakeet. Prior to the 6th of January, her pet parakeet was described as having a warm demeanor and often sought Louise's presence and comfort. However, overnight, just after their incident, the parakeet became hysterical whenever Louise entered the room and

---

[80] Walt Peters, "Louise Smith/Kentucky Women Abduction", *Factual Eyewitness Testimony of U.F.O. Encounters* (2013).

would only calm down when she left. Just a month later, the parakeet passed away. Although some may be quick to dismiss these changes and anomalies as mere coincidences, I do believe that there is more to it than that.

As word about their encounter continued to spread, Mona, Elaine, and Louise were approached by various media outlets and news reporters to talk about their experience, but they refused. At no point did the women seek publicity or money from the incident, they solely wanted an explanation. Things began to change when Jerry Black from MUFON reached out to them, and this marked the beginning of some shocking and disturbing revelations.

▲ ▼ ▲

The investigation
29th of February 1976

Jerry spoke with the women at length about their experience and he realized that he had seen this situation before. The physical ailments, psychological distress, mechanical anomalies, and missing time period were all components of a typical alien abduction, and this provided the women with some solace. They agreed to pursue a formal investigation under the guidance of MUFON, so they met on Sunday the 29th of February. On the day, Mona, Elaine, and Louise met with Jerry Black and Leonard Stringfield, another UFO researcher and prominent figure in the UFO field. As we shall find out, this investigation would reveal far more than what the women were anticipating or ready to face.

They started off by recounting the incident from the very start to the best of their recollection. They were visibly distraught, and this was evident throughout the conversation. They were still experiencing the burning sensations and Mona's eyes were also greatly inflamed, which corroborated their testimony. Out of the three women, Elaine was the most contained and so she did the majority of the talking. After describing the incident, she stated that they now lived in fear, and understandably so—they were still unaware of what had taken place and their health had deteriorated so drastically and rapidly following that night. Elaine also expressed her concern for Louise and Mona who were not coping well with the situation.

We live in fear of what we don't know. I'm worried about Lou and
Mona. I think they're ready for a breakdown.[81]

Jerry and Leonard were aware that all of these factors pointed towards
a potential alien abduction, and the way forward was to explore the
missing time period. They believed that by exploring what took place
during that time, the women would learn how they came to suffer from
these ailments. They were also hoping that this revelation would provide the women with some closure. Although this was an ideal case
for MUFON to investigate, Jerry knew that the more publicity the
women received, the more distress they were going to experience, so
the researchers agreed that they would not publicize the investigation
without their consent and approval.

Following the initial meeting, Jerry met with Dr. J. Allen Hynek for
a consultation and they agreed that the women were too distressed in
their current state to go over the night in question in detail. However,
they were hoping that by entering a hypnotic trance, they would be able
to access and retrieve memories that were simply too overwhelming
and distressing for them to bear and were thus suppressed from their
conscious mind. This was the reason why hypnotic regression was recommended, and so Mona agreed to undergo hypnosis.

Mona's hypnotic regression
7th March 1977

Mona met with psychologist Dr. Leonard Sprinkle on the 7th of March
1977. The plan was to guide Mona into a hypnotic trance and then carefully relive the events of the 6th of January. Going back to that evening,
Mona recalled how she was sitting in the back seat as Louise drove and
Elaine sat in the passenger's seat. Shortly into the drive, the women
noticed a bright light in the sky and initially they were intrigued by its
appearance, but it then began maneuvering erratically, moving from
side to side and making instantaneous accelerations with sudden halts.
Curiosity turned to apprehension as they noticed the bright light getting closer to the car, until it was close enough for them to see its salient
features.

---

[81] Leonard Stringfield, "The Stanford, Kentucky Abduction", *The MUFON UFO Journal*,
110 (1977).

It was an enormous disk-shaped aircraft with bright lights around its circumference. It was at that moment that the curiosity morphed into fear, and as it inched closer to the vehicle, the disk emitted an intense beam of light which illuminated the interior of the car and the entire road ahead. When the car's interior intensely lit up, a fog-like effect was produced; at that moment Mona, Elaine, and Louise felt a scorching pain all over their bodies. Then, everything went black. As Mona recounted this experience, she became extremely agitated and distressed, and Dr. Sprinkle guided her out of the hypnotic trance and grounded her back to the present moment. The session was intense, and Mona was emotionally and physically exhausted. In his notes, Dr. Sprinkle observed how "Mona was tearful and seemed exhausted."[82]

While Mona was regaining her composure in her seat, Leonard Stringfield sat next to her. In the file he was holding were several sketches and drawings of alien beings made by previous contactees. As Mona caught a glimpse of one of them, she stared at it and was taken aback—she was certain that she had seen that same creature! Although this was a pivotal discovery for Mona, Stringfield's suggestiveness must be criticized. By intentionally showing her a drawing of an alien being, he could have influenced the recollection of her memories, especially in such a vulnerable state.

> I can see the face now ... but it does not seem solid. It comes and goes. I mean, fades an reappears like in a fog. The eyes are far apart and at the bottom ... the chin ... is like that drawing.[83]

▲ ▼ ▲

Weeks continued to pass by, and Mona, Louise, and Elaine's health continued to deteriorate. Their lives did not show any signs of improvement; conversely, they continued to lose weight and had now started experiencing very vivid and discombobulated nightmares. The only form of support they received came from MUFON and APRO, but the two organizations were financially strained and were limited as to how much they could help them. Unfortunately, the organizations had reached a point where they were unable to continue funding the

---

[82] Ibid.
[83] Ibid.

investigation, but the women were still in dire need of help. Through-out those few weeks, Jerry maintained contact with them and he fortunately managed to reach an agreement with *The National Enquirer*—in exchange for exclusive coverage, the newspaper offered to pay for the entire cost of the investigation.

The polygraph test
23rd June 1976

The first step in the investigation was for Mona, Elaine, and Louise to each undergo a polygraph test as this would add to their credibility. On Wednesday the 23rd of June 1976, they met with James Young, a detective for the Lexington Police Department who administered the polygraph test separately for Mona, Elaine, and Louise. Throughout his questioning, he attempted to find gaps and inconsistencies in their story, and many times he insinuated they were fabricating the story, but each time they reiterated they were being truthful. Young concluded that Mona, Elaine, and Louise were telling the truth and believed that they had truly experienced what they had recounted.

> Young said that his subjects "breezed through" their incredible
> story and polygraphically came out of the tests as credible people.[84]

Hypnotic regression

The hypnotic regression sessions were a pivotal point in the investigation. Six months had now passed since their incident, which was hopefully enough time for the women to return to the night in question and recount the events without becoming too distressed. Dr. Sprinkle met with the three women separately, and this is what surfaced:

> Although it is not possible to claim absolutely that a physical exam-ination and abduction has taken place I believe that the tentative hypothesis of abduction and examination is the best hypothesis to explain the apparent loss-of-time experience, the apparent physical

---

[84] Ibid.

and emotional reactions of the witnesses to the UFO sighting: the anxiety and the reactions of the witnesses to their experiences which have occurred after their UFO sighting.[85]

Louise's hypnotic regression

After guiding Louise into a calm, hypnotic trance, Dr. Sprinkle took Louise back to the night of the 6th of January. Right after they finished their meal, they started their drive back home, but some minutes into the drive, Louise observed a bright light in the sky. She first thought that it was an aircraft about to crash, but it then started maneuvering erratically and approaching their vehicle. Once it was close enough for them to discern its characteristics, Louise noticed that it was a disk-shaped aircraft, and this sight was startling and "so frightening that it [was] hard to look at."[86]

In the driver's seat, Louise kept a close eye on the disk as it continued to maneuver erratically, inching closer and closer to the car. Shortly thereafter, through the rearview mirrors, Louise noticed that the disk was tailing their car, and suddenly she lost complete control over the vehicle. Things continued to spiral out of control; despite the fact that her foot was completely off the pedal, the car maintained its speed. Louise recounted how it felt as though the car was being tugged backwards. Following this, everything went black. Back in the room, Louise was crying hysterically, and what she recounted next was even more disturbing.

When Louise opened her eyes, she found herself lying on a table in what appeared to be an operating room. The room was bright, and as she looked around, she noticed several creatures looking down at her. Their appearance was grotesque: they were around four and a half foot tall with bulging, slanted, dark eyes and wore a dark, tight-fitted suit with a hood over their heads. Louise also noticed a pungent smell but was unaware of where it was coming from. As she lay still on the table, one of the creatures approached her and poured a scorching liquid all over her body. It was agonizing and suffocating, and she believed that she was going to die at that very moment. That was the last memory

---

[85] APRO, "The Kentucky Abduction", *The APRO Bulletin*, 24(6) (1976).
[86] Walt Peters, "Louise Smith/Kentucky Women Abduction", *Factual Eyewitness Testimony of U.F.O. Encounters* (2013).

Louise could recall. She said: "I thought I was going to die because I could not breathe. It was so hot."

The days following her hypnotic regression session with Dr. Sprinkle were arduous. Her condition took a turn for the worse and she often commented on how she would not live to see another birthday. She felt particularly anxious when she was left alone and she avoided it at all costs, to the point where she slept at her parents' or friends' houses. Interestingly, on the 1st of August, Louise felt compelled to return to the road where the incident had taken place, and there she felt an inexplicable urge to look down at her hands. It was then that she noticed that the three rings she always wore were missing. Several months later, much to her surprise, as she was walking outside her trailer, she found the three rings on the ground.

Mona's hypnotic regression

Mona was in the passenger seat for the ride home, and as Louise lost control of the car, she described how it felt like it was moving backwards. She grabbed the steering wheel, trying to help Louise regain control over the wheel, but somehow, even though Louise's foot was completely off the accelerator, the car continued to reverse rapidly until it came to a stop. Similar to Louise, Mona recounted how everything went black after that, and when she opened her eyes, she found herself lying on an examination table in a brightly lit room. She tried to sit up to see where she was, but she felt a force of some sort holding her down. It was then that she saw four or five creatures approaching her. The description she provided was very similar to Louise's—they were "short humanoids who sat around in surgical masks and surgical garments."[87]

The humanoids looked down at her and observed her closely. She felt completely immobilized and stuck to the table, and all she could do was stare at the aliens' bulging, dark eyes. After some moments, one of the creatures approached the table and poured a burning liquid over her face. There were no words to describe the fear and pain she felt at that moment, and Mona was reliving the experience once again in the room. She cried out in pain as the liquid covered her body. She also felt a pressure against her eyes. After a few moments, Mona described seeing what seemed to be a long and dark tunnel. At the end of this very long tunnel was a brightly lit room, and as she walked past it, through a small window she saw a

---

[87] APRO, "The Kentucky Abduction" The APRO Bulletin, 11(6) (1978).

woman lying on an examination table, but she was unable to identify who she was. These were the last memories Mona could recall.

Elaine's hypnotic regression

As the car started reversing rapidly, Elaine shouted in panic in the back seat. She described how Mona and Louise frantically tried to regain control over the car, but to no avail. Once the car came to a stop, she was separated from Louise and Mona and found herself inside a small room which she described as a "chamber with a window on the side."[88] Inside this room were several humanoid creatures moving back and forth, observing her closely.

The creatures were identical to the ones Louise and Mona described; they had a childlike frame with disproportionate heads and distinct eyes. The humanoids observed her closely as they walked back and forth, and after some time a boiling liquid was poured all over her body, causing her unbearable pain. Unfortunately, Elaine was subjected to a second gruesome experiment. The alien beings went on to place a material around her neck which tightened each time she tried to speak or think. This barbaric experiment went on for a few moments and each time a thought entered her mind, the material would tighten and suffocate her. As she recalled this experiment during the session, Elaine placed her hands around her neck and cried in despair.

After the material was removed from around her neck a second alien approached her and placed a small device, which looked like a one-inch bullet, over her left breast. As the encounter came to an end, Elaine explained how somehow, she knew that these experiments were conducted in order for these beings to explore emotional and intellectual processes in humans.

Hypotheses

Hypothesis #1: The extraterrestrial hypothesis

The material revealed under hypnosis provides us with a wealth of information on what took place during that hour and twenty minutes. If we look at the details Mona, Elaine, and Louise uncovered, there are

---

[88] Ibid.

two common denominators: the presence and description of the alien beings, and the nature of the experiments they were subjected to. The predominant detail of the encounter is the harrowing experiments, which all seemed to be revolved around the women's fear and pain response. This observation reaffirms a supposition I have been making throughout this book, that these extraterrestrial entities seem to be interested in how humans process emotions such as fear, anxiety, and pain.

The extraterrestrial hypothesis is corroborated by several factors, the biggest one being the immediate and intermediate aftereffects. Following their incident, Elaine, Mona, and Louise all experienced debilitating and acute symptoms: they each found a red mark behind their necks and all discovered burn marks around their bodies. Undoubtedly, the physiological and psychological symptoms are a testament to the trauma they endured, and this degree of suffering is not something that can be feigned. Aside from these symptoms, there were other immediate and intermediate aftereffects as well—the mechanical anomalies in Louise's car and watch, as well as the imminent death of her pet parakeet. The second factor which supports the extraterrestrial hypothesis is the women's intentions. At no point in their lives did Mona, Louise, or Elaine attempt to profit from their experiences or seek fame or publicity. On the contrary, they avoided the public as much as they possibly could; they solely wanted an explanation to what they were experiencing.

The third piece of evidence is the corroborating UFO reports which were made on the same night of the incident. On that night, several reports were made by numerous individuals who reported seeing bright lights in the sky and a disk-shaped aircraft. Interestingly, one of the reports was made by a couple who lived very close to the farm where Louise's car came to a halt. The couple described seeing a "large, luminous object, shaped like a light-bulb pass low over the Stanford area."[89] Another report was made by the owner of another nearby farm who observed a glow of bright, white light traveling at a low altitude. He went on to say that the object then emitted a bright white beam of light.

---

[89] Leonard Stringfield, "The Stanford, Kentucky Abduction", *The MUFON UFO Journal*, 110 (1977).

Hypothesis #2: A hoax

The only other hypothesis that makes sense in this context is that the women made up the entire story, although this theory directly contradicts the aforementioned mounting evidence.

Conclusion

If we analyze the details and evidence presented in this chapter, we can deduce two possible hypotheses: either the case is authentic and the women were indeed abducted by an alien entity, or else Louise, Mona, and Elaine fabricated the entire story. The former seems to be more plausible when taking account all the evidence we have. However, this conclusion implies that there is an extraterrestrial entity out there with "malicious" intentions and is particularly intrigued by the fear and pain response in humans. On the other hand, if this was a hoax, it would imply that all of the evidence we examined was merely coincidental, and this seems rather unlikely.

The narrative, detail, and evidence of this case make it one of the best documented cases of an alien abduction. Unfortunately for Mona, Elaine, and Louise, days turned into weeks, and weeks turned into years, and they continued to suffer from the immediate and intermediate aftereffects. Although they learned to cope better with the situation, they never returned to the women they were before the incident. Throughout the writing of this chapter I couldn't even fathom just how terrifying this experience must have been for these three women, and I have no doubt whatsoever that what they recounted was the truth.

CHAPTER 13

The hills' encounter

Date: 19th September 1961
Location: New Hampshire, United States

The Betty and Barney Hill abduction case was the first widely publicized and most well-documented account of an alien abduction to this day. This case has an abundance of evidence, and as we will see, it is easy to see why it is regarded as the most extraordinary account of a close encounter—in a way, you cannot study alien abductions without studying the Hills' case. Betty and Barney first met in the summer of 1956 and married four years later. It was 1960 and being in an interracial relationship was not easy and relatively uncommon in the United States. Having said that, both Betty and Barney were activists and fought for civil rights movements throughout their lives. Later in his life, Barney even sat on a local board for the Commission on Civil Rights.

The Hills resided in Portsmouth, New Hampshire, and Betty worked as a social worker while Barney worked for the postal service. Although they married in 1960, it wasn't until 1961 that they went on their honeymoon trip. It was September, and they planned on going to Montreal and Niagara Falls, with Barney doing the driving so that they could take their beloved dog Delsey with them. Their honeymoon trip was unforgettable indeed, but for reasons unbeknown to them at the time. What follows is the remarkable story of Betty and Barney Hill, the first documented alien abduction case.

▲ ▼ ▲

The honeymoon trip
19th September 1961

Betty and Barney had been married for over a year at this point, but life events, commitments, and the general rigors of daily life had kept them from going on their honeymoon trip earlier. The plan was for them to drive through Vermont to Niagara Falls, then on to Toronto and Montreal, taking Delsey with them, who they loved dearly and could not leave behind. It was Sunday the 17th of September when they left their home, and the first two days went smoothly, just as they had planned. This break was exactly what they needed. Things, however, took a turn on Tuesday the 19th, and as they would soon learn, this day marked the beginning of a new chapter in their lives.

As they were driving through Montreal, Barney made a wrong turn, but the road signs were all in French which he couldn't understand and thus he could not get back on track. It was getting dark and late, and after several hours of trying to figure out where they were, they decided it would be best if they just found a motel nearby that would accept Delsey, and then continue on their journey the following morning. The problem with that plan was twofold: finding a hotel that would accept Delsey was a challenge in itself, and being an interracial couple meant they faced a lot of prejudice and discrimination. Alas, they had no choice but to drive around and hope for the best. As they drove through the streets of Montreal, the radio station announced that storm Esther was heading towards New Hampshire, with winds as strong as 130 miles per hour. This meant that if they followed their itinerary, they would get caught in the middle of the storm. And so they agreed to cut the trip short so they could get home in time.

The drive back to Portsmouth was initially calm and quiet, with the brightly lit moon illuminating the clear, starry sky. However, this is when things started to take a turn ... as they drove through Indian Head, Betty noticed a bright light maneuvering just below the bright moon and Jupiter. The two celestial bodies were conspicuous, and Betty could clearly distinguish the maneuvering light from them, and as she pointed it out to Barney, he first presumed it was a meteorite or a satellite, but the light then came to a sudden halt and remained motionless for a few moments before it initiated a vertical climb.

> ... the Hills spotted a bright moving star-like object in the southwest sky. The sky was clear and brightly illuminated by a 10-day-old gibbous moon. The object moved from below the moon and the planet Jupiter, which were low in the sky.[90]

While Betty was taken aback and amazed by what she was seeing, Barney tried to provide a rational explanation for it. Alas, each explanation he considered was quickly dismissed as the light continued to move erratically from side to side. Surely, no aircraft, celestial body, or satellite could maneuver like that, and they were both aware of this. Betty asked Barney to pull the car over to the side of the road so they could get a better look at it. As Barney insisted that it must have been an airline aircraft, the light came to a halt once more, performed a 180-degree turn and started moving towards their direction; it was as though whoever was piloting it had spotted them. Barney's anxiety and apprehension began to rise at this point as he realized they were witnessing something unusual. He tried to conceal his concern from Betty, who, on the other hand, was intrigued by what she was seeing. He insisted that they return to the car and continue on their journey home.

> This maneuver puzzled Mr. Hill; no airliner should suddenly decide to change its course like that. It was almost as if the object had seen them and was coming over to investigate.[91]

Prior to their departure on Sunday, Barney placed the .32 caliber pistol they kept at home in the trunk of their car just in case they needed to protect themselves, and at that moment he felt threatened and wary, so he placed the pistol beneath his seat. They continued on with their drive. The light was still distinctly visible in the clear sky, and at this

---

[90] Walter Webb, "A Dramatic UFO Encounter in the White Mountains, New Hampshire, The Hill Case—Sept. 19–20, 1961," NICAP, September 1965, http://nicap.org/reports/610919hill_report2.pdf.
[91] Ibid.

point it was low and close enough for Betty and Barney to discern its characteristics. The light was a disk-shaped aircraft with bright lights around its rim, illuminating its smooth, metallic surface. The disk continued to perform erratic maneuvers completely silently, moving in a step-like pattern, climbing vertically, leveling off, and then dropping. As Betty and Barney looked in awe, they further noticed that the disk seemed to be spinning on its own axis.

At this point they were driving through Franconia Notch in the White Mountains, and the disk was behind the Cannon Mountains at an altitude of around 4,000 feet and just a mile ahead of them. Barney pulled the car to the side of the road again, but their view of the disk was obstructed by the trees, so they drove ahead past Indian Head where they found a clearing. There, they noticed that the disk's rim was only half lit; one half had flickering bright lights while the other was dark. The disk was also hovering just 100 feet above the ground and it was in close proximity; they estimated its size to be roughly the same as that of a large four-engined aircraft, and on each of its ends was a flickering red light. At its center was a row of windows with bright fluorescent light glowing from the inside. The disk continued to spin on its axis until at one moment it came to a halt and started to glide silently towards a nearby field, to the left of the highway.

> Barney Hill still believed what he was seeing had a rational explanation—a military helicopter perhaps having some fun with them. What amazed him though was the ease with which this craft seemed to move and stop and the absolute lack of any sound at this close range.[92]

Barney proceeded to grab the .32 caliber pistol and binoculars from the car and started walking towards the clearing, just where the disk was hovering, leaving Betty alone in the car with Delsey. As he reached the clearing, Barney's apprehension and fear took over, and the disk started to descend slowly. Looking through his binoculars he noticed a total of eleven figures standing at the windows, staring back at him, attentively. The figures looked humanoid and were wearing a gleaming black uniform with black caps, the material similar to leather. Their features were similar to a human's, and their presentation reminded

---

[92] Ibid.

Barney of a German SS officer. Barney continued to look through the binoculars as the disk hovered silently. Out of nowhere, he noticed a burst of energy inside, and all but one of the humanoid beings scurried away.

Back in the car, Betty was growing restless as she waited for Barney to return. After a few minutes she saw him running towards the car in a panic, visibly distraught and repeating to himself that he could not believe what he had just seen. He also kept murmuring that they were about to get captured. He started the car and pressed his foot on the accelerator, speeding as fast as the car could possibly go. They were now driving along Route 3, and Barney was still repeating the same sentence over and over in a panic. Shortly thereafter, they started hearing a buzzing noise inside the car, which faded after a few seconds.

> [Betty] appeared more concerned with her husband's safety than with watching the UFO, said he dashed toward the car, laughing or crying hysterically and repeating "They're going to capture us."[93]

The buzzing noise returned, and the interior of the car was now vibrating. Ahead of them they noticed a bright light in the middle of the road, and it seemed just like a roadblock. This brought relief to Betty and Barney as they thought there were other human beings nearby and were no longer alone. However, as they drove closer, they noticed that the bright orange light was obstructing the road, and this was the last thing they consciously recalled before arriving home in Portsmouth several hours later.

▲ ▼ ▲

The aftermath

The drive back home should have taken around two hours, which meant that they should have arrived at around 03:00, however, it took them twice as long and they arrived at 05:00. As they walked through the front door, the first thing they did was walk to the window and look up at the sky. They both acknowledged that they had seen a

---

[93] Ibid.

disk-shaped aircraft, but they were unaware that there was more to the story than what they could consciously recall. It is important to note that at this time, flying saucers, UFOs, and the paranormal in general were considered particularly taboo, and those who discussed them were frequently ridiculed. Barney wanted to avoid this, so after deliberating with Betty, they agreed that they would not mention their sighting to anyone. While Betty had initially agreed to this, as the hours passed, she became more curious and wanted to learn more about what they had witnessed.

Later in the morning, Betty phoned her sister Janet, who, around ten years earlier, had mentioned to her that she had seen a UFO herself. Surely if anyone would have understood Betty it would have been her, and she felt comfortable enough to confide in her. As she told Janet what they had seen the night before, Janet spoke to her neighbor, who happened to be a physicist, and he recommended they conduct a simple experiment using a compass to check for a magnetic field. Janet also spoke with a friend of hers who was a chief police officer, who recommended they make a formal report to Pease Air Force Base.

As Betty hung up the phone, she quickly found a compass and ran outside to their car. As she started approaching it, she noticed that there were several silver spots, the size of a half-dollar, all over its surface. Betty was certain they hadn't been there the day before as they surely would have noticed if they were. Furthermore, as she moved the compass over the spots, the needle started spinning. Betty ran back inside the house and shouted for Barney to go down and witness what was happening. The compass continued to spin, and even their neighbor was bewildered by this. Betty phoned Janet again and informed her of the outcome. Janet, together with her husband Don and their three children, drove to Betty and Barney's house where they saw the silver spots and carried out the experiment for themselves.

Betty and Barney recounted their sighting to them, though Barney omitted the part where he saw the humanoid beings on board the disk. It was at this point that Betty noticed that her and Barney's watches had stopped working at the exact same time. Although it is very common for wind-up watches to stop working, it is certainly odd that they did so simultaneously, at the same exact minute. Furthermore, even after they wound the watches up, they did not resume working.

▲ ▼ ▲

The investigation

The presence of the silver spots on the car, the compass experiment, and the strange mechanical failure in the watches indicated that something unusual had indeed occurred the previous night, and despite Barney's hesitation, Betty called Pease Air Force Base to file a formal report. At the 100th Bomb Wing at Pease Air Force Base, Betty spoke with Major Paul Henderson who spoke with the Hills at length. Once again, during the conversation, Barney omitted his part of the sighting where he saw the occupants of the disk. The following day, Major Henderson called Betty and Barney and informed them that he had written a report and had forwarded it to Project Blue Book for further investigation.

The Air Force report

Major Henderson's full report reads as follows:

A. Description of Object
　　1. Continuous band of lights—cigar shaped at all times despite changes of direction.
　　2. Size: When first observed it appeared to be about the size of a nickel at arm's length. Later when it seemed to be a matter of hundreds of feet above the automobile it would be about the size of a dinner plate held at arm's length.
　　3. Color: Only color evident was that of the band of lights when was comparable to the intensity and color of a filament of an incandescent lamp.
　　4. Number: One.
　　5. Formation: None.
　　6. Features or details: See 1 above. During period of observation wings seemed to appear from the main body. Described as V shaped with red lights on tips. Later, wings appeared to extend further.
　　7. Tail, trail or exhaust: None observed.
　　8. Sounds: None except as described in item E.
B. Description of course of Object.
　　1. First observed through windshield of car. Size and brightness of object compares to visible stars attracted observers' attention.
　　2. Angle of elevation, first observed: About 45 degrees.

    3. Angle of elevation at disappearance: Not determinable because of inability to observe its departure from the auto.

    4. Flight path & maneuvers: See item E.

    5. How object disappeared: See item E.

    6. Length of observation: Approx. 30 mins.

C. Manner of Observation

    1. Ground-visual.

    2. Binoculars used at times.

    3. Sighting made from inside auto. while moving and stopped. Observed from within and outside auto.

[D. absent from the official document]

E. Location and details: On the night of 19–20 September between 20/0001 and 20/0100 the observers were traveling by car in a southerly direction on Route 3 south of Lincoln, N.H., when they noticed a brightly lighted object ahead of their car at an angle of elevation of approximately 45 degrees. It appeared strange to them because of its shape and the intensity of its lights compared to the stars in the sky. Weather and sky were clear. They continued to observe the moving object from their moving car for a few minutes, then stopped. After stopping the car, they used binoculars at times.

> They report that the object was traveling north very fast. They report it changed directions rather abruptly and then headed south. Shortly thereafter, it stopped and hovered in the air. There was no sound evident up to this time. Both observers used the binoculars at this point. While hovering, objects began to appear from the body of the "object," which they describe as looking like wings, which made a V-shape when extended. The "wings" had red lights on the tips. At this point they observed it to appear to swoop down in the general direction of their auto. The object continued to descend until it appeared to be only a matter of "hundreds of feet" above their car.
>
> At this point they decided to get out of that area, and fast. Mr. Hill was driving, and Mrs. Hill watched the object by sticking her head out the window. It departed in a generally northwesterly direction, but Mrs. Hill was prevented from observing its full departure by her position in the car.
>
> They report that while the object was above them after it had "swooped down" they heard a series of short, loud "buzzes,"

which they described as sounding like someone had dropped a tuning fork. They report that they could feel these buzzing sounds in their auto. No further visual observation was made of this object. They continued on their trip and when they arrived in the vicinity of Ashland, N.H., about 30 miles from Lincoln, they again heard the "buzzing" sound of the "object"; however, they did not see it at this time.

Mrs. Hill reported the flight pattern of the "object" to be erratic; [it] changed directions rapidly, [and] during its flight it ascended and descended numerous times very rapidly. Its flight was described as jerky and not smooth.

Mr. Hill is a civil service employee in the Boston Post Office and doesn't possess any technical or scientific training. Neither does his wife.

During a later conversation with Mr. Hill, he volunteered the observation that he did not originally intend to report the incident but in as much as he and his wife did in fact see this occurrence, he decided to report it. He says that on looking back he feels that the whole thing is incredible, and he feels somewhat foolish—he just cannot believe that such a thing could or did happen. He says, on the other hand, that they both saw what they reported, and this fact gives it some degree of reality.

Information contained herein was collected by means of telephone conversation between the observers and the preparing individual. The reliability of the observer cannot be judged, and while his apparent honesty and seriousness appears to be valid, it cannot be judged at this time.[94]

Corroborative sightings

Aside from the Hills' eyewitness testimony, the "Additional Item" section of the report is an imperative part of the Air Force document as it corroborates their encounter even further. In this section, Major Henderson reports that on the same day of their sighting, an unidentified target was tracked on radar at Pease Air Force Base:

---

[94] Paul Henderson, "Air Intelligence Information Report: 100-1-61—Unidentified Flying Object" (Sep 20, 1961).

During a casual conversation on 22 Sept 61 between Major Gardiner
B. Reynolds, 100th B W DCOI and Captain Robert O. Daughaday,
Commander 1917-2 AACS DIT, Pease AFB, NH it was revealed that
a strange incident occurred at 0214 local on 20 Sept. No importance
was attached to the incident at the time. Subsequent interrogation
failed to bring out any information in addition to the extract of the
"Daily Report to the Controller." Copy of this extract is attached. It is
not possible to determine any relationship between these two observations, as the radar observation provides no description. Time and
distance between the events could hint of a possible relationship.[95]

The extract Major Henderson is referring to is included hereunder,
signed by Captain Commander Robert Daughaday:

0614Z (this refers to the time, 02:14) observed unidentified A/C
(aircraft) come on PAR (precision approach radar) (4 miles out).
Aircraft made approach and pulled up at 1/2 a mile. Shortly after
observed, weak target on downwind, then when it made low
approach TWR (tower) unable to see any aircraft at any time.[96]

Furthermore, a second radar sighting was made just a few hours prior
at North Concord Air Force Station in Vermont.

Return on H/F (height-finder) radar size of a/c (aircraft) appearing
as normal target at 62,000 appeared 196 deg. at 84 mi, lost on contact 199 deg. at 80 mi, going NW then S and gradually S on scope
18 min.
    11. Comments: Relative low speed and high altitude coupled
with erratic course including weather balloon.
    12. Conclusion: Probably balloon.

The target performed erratic maneuvers, and while the conclusion
stated that the aircraft was a weather balloon, this seems highly unlikely.
It should be noted that the vast majority of UAP reports during this time
period were given the same explanation, which usually was that the

---

[95] Project Blue Book, National Archives—T-1206—Case 10073.
[96] Ibid.

reported UFO was either a misidentified weather balloon or a natural phenomenon.

The Air Force's conclusion

The Air Force's conclusion regarding the Betty and Barney Hill abduction case has changed twice over the years. In the original report published in September of 1961, Major Henderson concluded that the lights observed were advertising lights and that the unidentified, disk-shaped aircraft was a natural phenomenon. What phenomenon he was referring to, however, he did not specify. In that same conclusion, Major Henderson also reported that the radar sighting made at Pease Air Force Base was unrelated to the Hills' sighting and was the result of a temperature inversion.

> Both radar and visual sighting are probably due to conditions resulting from strong inversion which prevailed in area on morning of sighting. Actual source of light viewed is not known but it has all the characteristics of an advertising searchlight. Radar probably was looking at some ground target due to strong inversion (a temperature inversion can take place in a perfectly clear sky). No evidence indicating objects were due to other than natural causes.
>   12. Conclusions: Optical condition.[97]

Let us look at the first claim: that the bright, maneuvering light which Betty and Barney saw were advertising lights. Advertising lights are typically seen at public events and move from side to side at a low speed, making them easily distinguishable. This description does not correspond to Betty and Barney's narrative. The second claim was that the disk-shaped aircraft was a natural phenomenon, but he did not elaborate on what that phenomenon was—I personally am unaware of any natural phenomena which manifest as flying saucers.

After Major Henderson's conclusion in the Project Blue Book report, the Air Force released a second statement pertaining to the Hills case.

---

[97] Ibid.

This time, the Air Force concluded that the aircraft was in all probability, Jupiter:

> Information on Barney Hill sighting, 20 September 1961, Lincoln, New Hampshire. The Barney Hill sighting was investigated by officials from Pease AFB. The case is carried as insufficient data in the Air Force files. No direction (azimuth) was reported and there are inconsistencies in the report. The sighting occurred about midnight and the object was observed for at least one hour. No specific details on maneuverability were given. The planet Jupiter was in the South West, at about 20 degrees elevation and would have set at the approximate time that the object disappeared. Without positional data the case could not be evaluated as Jupiter. There was a strong inversion in the area. The actual light source is not known. As no lateral or vertical movement was noted, the object was in all probability Jupiter. No evidence was presented to indicate that the object was due to other than natural causes.[98]

This report contains several inconsistencies and incorrect details that the Hills did not report. For instance, the report mentions that the aircraft was observed for an hour whereas Betty and Barney only reported seeing it for half an hour. It then goes on to state that the Hills did not provide accurate details of the aircraft's maneuverability, even though they did. If we look at the aforementioned details in this chapter and the initial Air Force report, one can see that they did indeed provide an accurate description of what they witnessed. Lastly, the report concludes that the aircraft was most likely Jupiter. This conclusion does not hold true for several reasons: to start with, when Betty originally saw the bright light maneuvering, she was able to identify both the moon and Jupiter. In fact, the bright light was maneuvering beneath the two celestial bodies. Furthermore, if the light had been Jupiter, then it would not have performed the maneuvers the Hills described seeing.

---

[98] William Brummett and Ernest Zuick, "Should the USAF Reopen Project Blue Book?" (Dissertation, Air University, Maxwell Air Force Base, 1974).

Betty's nightmares

Back at the Hills' residence, up until that point, neither Betty nor Barney had any indication that they had been captured by an extraterrestrial entity. All they could consciously recall was seeing the disk maneuvering erratically and arriving home much later than expected. However, things began to change ten days after their encounter, when Betty started experiencing vivid nightmares that were both obscure and horrifying. She experienced these dreams for five days in a row, and as they persisted, she told Barney about them, but he told her not to dwell on them as they were just dreams. Following his comment, Betty stopped discussing them with him and started keeping a dream journal instead, in which she wrote down in detail the content of her dreams. Before we delve into Betty's dream journals, I should point out that the timeline of Betty's dreams was often disorganized and jumbled. Having said that, the events are presented in this chapter in a coherent and chronological order to help the reader follow and understand the timeline of events more easily. Furthermore, since Betty described the beings as men, they will be alluded to as such and will be referred to using the masculine pronouns.

Betty's nightmares begin at the bottom of a well where everything is dark. She looks around, and as she tries to crawl out of the well, she struggles to stay awake and lucid. The next thing she notes in her journal, she is in the middle of a dark wooded area; the surrounding trees are blocking the moonlight, but from afar she can see a light source which is emitting a bright glow. Surrounding Betty is a group of men. Barney is with her in the woods, and he too is surrounded by a group of men; however, his eyes are shut. Betty yells at him to wake up, but he remains unresponsive as they are guided toward the light source ahead.

> ... next to me on both sides is a man; two men in the front; two men in the back; then Barney with a man on each side of him; other men in back of his.[99]

The men surrounding Betty and Barney are around five to five and a half feet tall. They have anthropomorphic features, with large chests, a gray-toned complexion and bluish lips, dark hair and eyes, and

---

[99] Betty Hill, "Dreams or Recall?" (Durham, NH: University of New Hampshire Library, 1961).

prominent, large noses. They are all dressed in the same uniform which consists of a hat, a pair of boots and trousers (this description matches the one Barney gave of the occupants he saw through the binoculars in the middle of the clearing). Although their appearance is eerie, throughout her journals Betty reiterates that at no point did she feel threatened or unsafe. They continue to walk through the dark woods, approaching the light source. The man to Betty's left tells her that they will not be harmed and that they will be returned safely to their car after they carry out some medical experiments. The creature speaks to Betty in broken English, and he goes on to ask her what her husband's name is, but she refuses to answer. As they reach the light source, Betty notices that the glow was emanating from the large disk which was in the center of the clearing. The disk is enormous, roughly the size of a house and has a smooth metallic surface with a ramp leading to the inside.

> Barney is all right; no harm will come to us. All they want to do is make some tests; when these are completed in a very brief time, they will take us back to the car and we will go safely on our way home. We have nothing to fear.[100]

Betty tries resisting, but the men have a firm grip on her and continue to guide her up the ramp. As they enter the disk, Betty observes how it feels cold, and ahead of her is a long corridor. Barney is still being held by the group of men with his eyes shut, and is taken further down the corridor while Betty is taken to the first room, which is bright and bare except for an examination table in the center. Two beings then enter the room, one of whom is the same being who spoke to Betty as they were walking in the woods and the other introduces himself as the examiner. Betty refers to the first being as the "leader." The examiner proceeds to approach Betty and starts by inquiring about her and Barney's ages. He then asks her about their nutrition and what they consume. After this, the examiner explains that they will be conducting a few medical experiments to help them determine the differences between humans and their species.

> Then the examiner said that he wished to do some tests to find out the basic differences between him and us; that I would not be harmed in any way and would not experience pain.[101]

---

[100] Ibid.
[101] Ibid.

The examiner starts off by collecting some samples, including her hair, fingernails, and earwax. He also examines her mouth, throat, and ears. Lastly, he withdraws an instrument and with it he scrapes Betty's arms and places the skin sample onto a clear plastic slide. Once the examiner finishes collecting the samples, he explains how the next experiment will be centered upon the nervous system. As Betty is placed on the table, he starts taking off her blue dress but struggles to unzip it, causing a tear near the zipper region. He then brings over a device which looks similar to an EEG machine. This instrument is placed over Betty's head and with a needle he touches various parts of her body.

The examiner tells Betty that the final experiment is very similar to a pregnancy test. He brings over a long needle and places it into her navel. This causes an excruciating pain unlike anything she had ever felt before, and when the leader notices her discomfort, he walks over and places his hands in front of her face, causing the pain to dissipate instantly. As the final experiment is concluded, the examiner leaves the room, leaving Betty alone with the leader, whom she feels a sense of gratitude towards. Before they start talking, a group of men rush into the room and start communicating with the leader. He then follows the group outside the room and once he returns, he starts examining Betty's mouth, tugging at her teeth. At that moment Betty assumed what might have happened: as they were examining Barney's teeth, his dentures must have fallen out.

As Betty looks around the room, she realizes what an unfathomable experience this is and how everyone back home would certainly not believe her when she told them. For this reason, she asks the leader if she could take a memento with her from the disk back home, and he does not object to this. As she continues to look around the room, a large book catches her eyes, and as she opens it, she sees that it is written in indecipherable symbols. This leads Betty to ask about their origin, and to answer her question, the leader walks over to the wall and pulls down a map which is covered in white specks. Connecting these white specks are lines, some dotted and others solid. The leader then asks Betty if she can find Earth on the map, and when she says she can't, he tells her that it was thus futile to show her if she couldn't decipher the map to start with.

> It was a map of the heavens, with numerous size stars and planets, some large, some only pinpoints. Between many of these, lines were dawn, some broken lines, some light solid lines, some heavy black lines. They were not straight but curved. Some went from one

planet to another, to another, in a series of lines. Others had no lines
and he said the lines were expeditions.[102]

After a few moments, Barney appears at the door surrounded by the
group of men, and the pair are then escorted outside the disk. As
they are being escorted towards their car, Betty hears some commo-
tion behind her, and she sees the leader in discussion with the rest of
the group; the leader then approaches Betty and takes the book from
her, explaining how the rest of the group had objected to her having
proof of the encounter. Betty is infuriated at this and tells the leader
that regardless of whether she has the book or not, she will still remember the details and the encounter. The leader responds, telling her that
was unlikely and that they would do everything possible to make her
forget, but even if she did remember, Barney would not. As Betty and
Barney are returned to their car, they find Delsey under the front seat,
trembling with fear. The beings then return to the disk, and as the bright
glow intensifies, the aircraft lifts from the ground and makes a rapid
vertical ascent out of view.

> I became very angry and said that somehow, somewhere, I would
> remember; that there was nothing he could do to make me forget
> this. He laughed and agreed that I might possibly do just that—to
> remember, but he would do his best to prevent me from this.[103]

I must emphasize once more that, while the events were presented
chronologically and coherently, the way she wrote them in her dream
journals was not. They were simply written in this manner to facilitate
the reader's reading experience.

▲ ▼ ▲

Addressing the missing time

Betty continued to experience these vivid nightmares for nights on
end, but she did not share them with Barney—she only wrote them
in her journals. Furthermore, it is worth noting that although she was

---

[102] Ibid.
[103] Ibid.

experiencing these dreams, at this point she did not comprehend that they had been abducted by aliens. With the confusion she felt, she desperately sought answers, so she visited the local library where she started reading books related to the UFO phenomenon. At the end of one of these books was Donald Keyhoe's address, one of the most prominent researchers in the field of UFOs. Betty wrote Keyhoe a letter detailing their encounter and everything they had been experiencing since then, and around a month later she received a reply, telling her that he would like to meet her and Barney. On the 21st of October 1961, Betty and Barney met with Donald Keyhoe, Walter Webb, the director of NICAP, and Major James McDonald. The group met at the Hills' residence, and they related their encounter once more.

Aside from experiencing nightmares, Betty reported feeling anxious and tense, which was not something she had ever experienced for an extended period of time in the past. Furthermore, as a result of their encounter, Barney began experiencing physiological and psychological symptoms, including anxiety and insomnia. He also had to visit the doctor several times due to ulcers and high blood pressure. In addition to these symptoms, he discovered a ring of warts in his groin region that had to be surgically removed. After talking with the Hills at length, it was recommended that they undergo hypnotic regression to further explore what happened that night. Betty and Barney agreed, and the hypnotic regression sessions took place in 1964.

The Hills met with Dr. Benjamin Simon on numerous occasions between January and June 1964. Dr. Simon was a highly experienced psychiatrist who had previously worked with World War II veterans, and the Hills underwent hypnosis separately. Before we go into the hypnosis sessions, it is important to note that at the end of each session, Dr. Simon placed both of them in a state of amnesia, in which they would be unable to recall what they had uncovered during the session. This is crucial since it ensured that they did not share the details with one another as this would have undoubtedly influenced the other's narrative.

In the first session, Dr. Simon spent eight hours guiding the Hills into a deep, hypnotic trance, and it was at this deepest level that they were able to access the repressed memories which were being kept from their conscious state. The following details are presented as a single cohesive event, but they were recounted over a period of six months. To avoid repetition, I will be omitting the first part of the sighting which includes the details that the Hills could consciously recall. The narrative will pick up with Barney observing the disk in the middle of the clearing.

Barney's hypnosis

> It looks like a big, big pancake with windows and rows of windows and lights, not lights, just like one big light.[104]

As Barney stood in the middle of the clearing, he had a clear and unobstructed view of the disk, which was hovering silently just a few feet away. Through his binoculars he saw a group of men standing at the window, staring back at him. They were dressed like a group of German SS soldiers, with a dark black shirt, a jacket, a black scarf and hat. Their dark, slanted eyes were fixated on him, and after a few moments, Barney noticed a burst of energy inside and all the men hurried away except for one. The being who remained at the window continued to stare at Barney and they locked eyes with each other. At that instant, he heard a foreign voice in his head, a telepathic message telling him not to be afraid as they were not going to be harmed. The look in the creature's eyes was chilling and mesmerizing—it was an indescribable feeling, and just by the look, Barney could tell that these beings were extraterrestrials. During the hypnotic regression session, as Barney described the feeling and the being's eyes, he became increasingly anxious and distressed.

Dr. Simon grounded Barney back to the present moment and reassured him that he was safe. They then went back to the night of the encounter, and Barney continued to recount how he then started running back towards the car, where Betty and Delsey were waiting for him. He rushed to the driver's seat and slammed the accelerator as hard as he could. As they sped down Route 3, they noticed a bright orange light in the middle of the road and a group of men motioning for him to pull over to the side. This was reassuring at first as he assumed it was a roadblock and that there were other humans nearby, but as they got closer, he realized that these were not people after all, but the same creatures he had seen on board the disk in the clearing just a few minutes earlier.

A group of six men started approaching the car, all dressed in the same attire, the same outfit Barney had described. As they continued to

---

[104] "Hypnosis Session 1", (Durham, NH: University of New Hampshire Library, 1961).

approach the vehicle, Barney felt compelled to close his eyes, as though he was told to do so, and he kept them closed until he saw a bright white light. As he opened his eyes, he found himself in what seemed to be an operating room. The room was illuminated by bright fluorescent lights and he lay upon a metallic table which was in the center of the room. One of the men took off his shoes and drew his pants down and proceeded to insert an instrument which had the same length and thickness of a pencil inside his rectum. Throughout all of this, Barney kept his eyes closed and remained quiet, even though he was utterly petrified. He knew that the more he kept quiet and the less he resisted, the sooner this would all be over.

> I was lying on the table and my fly was open and I thought "Are they putting a cup around my private parts?" And then it stopped, and I thought "If I keep real quiet and real still I won't be harmed."[105]

After they took a sample of his stool, the examiner proceeded to count his spinal column, putting pressure at the base of the spine. He then turned Barney over and examined his mouth and scraped his arms with an instrument which was akin to a letter opener. The final experiment was just as intrusive as the first one; the examiner approached Barney with a cup-like device and placed it against his genitals, and he held the device there for a couple of seconds.

> And I am not in pain. And I can feel a slight feeling. My groin feels cold.[106]

After the experiments came to an end, Barney was escorted outside the disk and placed in the car with Betty. Betty and Barney just stared at each other in disbelief as the creatures entered the disk. Immediately thereafter, the disk started ascending from the ground, getting brighter and more intense, and in an instant, it shot up towards the sky and disappeared.

> It was a bright huge ball ... It was a beautiful bright ball. And it was going, and it was gone, and we were in darkness.[107]

---

[105] "Hypnosis Session 2", (Durham, NH: University of New Hampshire Library, 1961).
[106] Ibid.
[107] Ibid.

Betty's hypnosis

As Dr. Simon guided Betty into a hypnotic trance, she described how Barney was overwrought and kept repeating to himself that they were going to be captured. A few miles ahead of them they saw a bright light in the middle of the road and assumed that this was a roadblock. As a group of men started approaching the car, they motioned for Barney to pull over to the side, and the closer they got, the more they realized that these individuals were not human beings after all. The group divided into two: one approached Barney's side while the other approached Betty's. Barney was now hysterical and was desperately trying to start the car's engine, but to no avail. As the group reached the vehicle, Betty recalled how she received a telepathic message, telling her that they would not be harmed and would be safely returned to the car. Despite their sinister and ghastly appearance, Betty felt rather safe.

> You don't have any reason to be afraid. We're not going to harm you. We just want to do some tests, and when the tests are over with, we'll take you and Barney back and put you in your car and you'll be on your way back home in no time.[108]

The group of men started escorting Betty out of the car and towards the bright glow. As she looked back at Barney, she saw that he was in a complete daze with his eyes closed. It was as though he was sleepwalking. As they got closer to the bright light, Betty observed how this was in actual fact the disk-shaped aircraft they had seen earlier, and in the center of the disk was a ramp leading to the inside. While Barney was led down the hallway, Betty was escorted into a different room. Into the room entered two beings, the examiner and the other one, whom Betty referred to as the leader. The examiner placed Betty on the metallic table and pushed up the sleeves of her blue dress. With an instrument which looked like a letter opener he scraped her skin and placed the sample on a clear plastic slide. He then placed her head on a bracket and examined her eyes, throat, and ears before taking an earwax sample. He ran his fingers through her hair, cut a few strands and placed them on another clear slide. Lastly, he examined behind her ears, neck, and shoulders and took a few fingernail clippings. Once the examiner

---

[108] "Hypnosis Session 3", (Durham, NH: University of New Hampshire Library, 1961).

finished collecting these samples, he informed her that they would be carrying out some experiments which would help them explore the differences between human beings and their species.

Betty was still on the table, and the examiner tried to unzip her dress, but he struggled to do so, causing a tear at the zipper region. This detail is a crucial part of the story, as will be revealed later on. He then brought over a device which looked similar to an EEG machine, except it lacked the machine and at the end of each wire was a needle. The examiner proceeded to touch different parts of her body with a needle and seemed particularly interested in the body's reflexes. After this, the examiner told Betty that they would be carrying out one final examination which was very similar to a pregnancy test. He reached over for an instrument which seemed to be a very long needle, around six inches long. He proceeded to place this needle inside her navel, thrusting it deep inside her. This caused an excruciating pain, a pain which she had never felt before. The leader was observing the examinations in the background, but as he noticed her discomfort, he walked over to her and placed his hands in front of her face, causing the pain to subside instantly. Once this final experiment was concluded, the examiner left the room, leaving her alone with the leader. Betty felt grateful to him and safe in his presence.

Betty began by telling him that no one back home would believe her if she told them what they had experienced, so she asked if she could take something from the room with her as proof. He did not object, but the room was relatively bare. She looked around and noticed a large book and as she opened it, she observed how it was written in indecipherable symbols assorted in short lines, some of which were dotted while others were straight and curved. This prompted Betty to ask the leader about their origin, and to answer her question he walked over to one of the walls and pulled down a map. The map was wide and oblong shaped, and it was covered in white specks of different sizes, some as small as a pinpoint while others were as large as a nickel. Connecting these dots were different lines, some of which were heavy and straight and others dotted. The leader went on to explain how the lines represented expeditions. He then asked her if she could locate Earth on it, and when she told him that she could not, he pulled it back up and told her it was irrelevant to show her if she could not understand the map to start with.

Their conversation was interrupted by a group of men who rushed into the room and started communicating with the leader in intelligible noises. The leader left the room for some moments and then, as he returned, he started examining Betty's mouth, tugging at her teeth. Betty then assumed that Barney's dentures had most probably fallen out which had puzzled the examiner, so she explained to the leader what dentures were and how losing teeth is a natural part of the aging process. She also explained how dental hygiene is greatly affected by nutrition and how humans consume mainly meat and vegetables. The leader inquired further about this, but he did not seem to grasp the concept of aging, or what meat and vegetables were.

After a few moments, Barney returned at the door with two men holding him from both of his sides. As they were being escorted outside the disk, Betty heard a discussion behind her and she saw the leader discussing something with the rest of the group in intelligible noises. Following this, the leader approached Betty and took back the large book she had taken from the room; he explained how the group had decided against her having evidence of the encounter. This angered Betty, who insisted that she would recall everything nonetheless. The leader replied, telling her that that was highly unlikely, but even if she did, the majority of people would not believe such an implausible and preposterous story. As the Hills were placed back in their car the disk transformed into a bright orange glow and shot up towards the sky. They arrived back home in Portsmouth at around 05:00, two hours after their estimated arrival.

Comments on the hypnotic regression sessions

The first observation I must mention is the similarity between the material in Betty's dream journals and the details which she recounted under hypnotic regression. Aside from a few differences, the narrative is almost identical. Although many have questioned how her nightmares could have been so detailed and accurate, it should be noted that traumatic events frequently resurface in dreams. When a person experiences a trauma, these memories are often kept from the conscious mind, which is why trauma survivors frequently do not recall the event. With that being said, it is common for these memories to surface while the individual is sleeping.

Moving on to the material uncovered from the hypnosis sessions, Betty and Barney's narratives are consistent and corroborate one another's. They each provide similar descriptions of the beings and the interior of the disk and were both subjected to intrusive medical experiments. If we look back at Betty's abduction, she recounted how the final experiment was similar to a pregnancy test and consisted of a large needle being inserted into her navel. This procedure is very similar to an amniocentesis, which is a medical procedure in which a sample of amniotic fluid is taken from the amniotic sac. Skeptics have argued that Betty described this procedure purposefully to further consolidate her narrative, but I highly doubt this was the case. This procedure was first recalled by Betty in 1961 in her dream journal, and back then, the procedure was very much in its infancy and was relatively new to the medical field. We must also keep in mind that Betty was a social worker, and the vast majority of people who would have known about the procedure would have in all likelihood worked in the medical field. The other detail which corroborates their testimony is the fact that following their encounter, Barney discovered growths in his groin region which had to be surgically removed. The growths formed a perfect circle, which corresponds to what he recalled while under hypnosis.

▲ ▼ ▲

The star map

Both in her dream journal and the hypnosis sessions, Betty mentioned that on board the disk she was shown a star map. During the hypnosis session with Dr. Simon during which she mentioned the star map, Dr. Simon told Betty that she would remember it exactly as she had seen it on board, and once she arrived home, he instructed her to relax and then reproduce a sketch of the map. Betty did just that, and her sketch consisted of twelve dots of different sizes connected by solid and dotted lines. Two of the twelve dots are noticeably larger than the rest and are adjoined by a band of five lines. Once Betty drew the map, she forwarded it to Dr. Simon, but after that she did not think much of it. Two years later, after reading about the Hills' encounter, Marjorie Fish, an elementary school teacher with an interest in astronomy contacted Betty and told her that she would be attempting to identify the star map.

The method

Fish's method to identify the star map was rigorous and took her several years. She first started by translating data she obtained from star catalogues and then created a three-dimensional model of the volume of space surrounding the sun. This process was meticulous and complex, and it is admittedly difficult to follow, but I will try to describe the method as concisely as possible. There are two terms which Fish used to select the data, F8 and K1. The former, according to astronomer Carl Sagan, refers to the point in the universe at which intelligent life may emerge, whereas the latter refers to the range of stars which are most suitable for the evolution of life.

From Betty and Barney's narrative, it was evident that these beings were intelligent and conscious beings, and thus, Fish restricted the range of stars to those between F8 and K1. This selection included stars in the solar system which are very similar to the Sun and could sustain the evolution of intelligent life. This process did not happen overnight or in a week. It took her several years to first obtain the star catalogues which she used to compare stars in patterns, another two years to locate what she thought were the first five stars in Betty's sketch, another eight months to locate the next four stars and another three years to identify the remaining three stars in the sketch.

In 1972, eight years into her project, Fish contacted Betty to inform her that she thought Zeta Tucanae was the prime candidate for the tenth star in the map, and although this was a massive breakthrough in the project, it did not quite match up with Betty's sketch of the map. Fish analyzed the star pattern from every possible angle, and lo and behold, the full sequence unfolded when she viewed it from below at a forty-five-degree angle. It was then that Fish realized that when viewed from just above Zeta II, the star pattern revealed itself in its entirety, which made her come to the conclusion that the star map she was shown on board the disk was that as seen from Zeta Reticulum.

Zeta Reticulum

This was a big discovery, and if it is indeed the case that these beings originated from Zeta Reticulum, then this naturally would imply that this star system can sustain the evolution of intelligent and conscious life-forms ... but how plausible is this? Zeta Reticulum is a binary star system in the constellation Reticulum which is approximately thirty-nine light years from Earth. The two stars, Zeta I and Zeta II are solar analogs, solar twins, meaning that they possess similar characteristics to the Sun. Moreover, the composition of Zeta Tucanae is also very similar to the Sun, and it is these similarities which lead many people to believe that this star system can indeed sustain the evolution of intelligent life.

The stars that make up the pattern in the Fish model fulfill the above exobiological criteria. For example, the lines in the map connect stars that are exclusively the type defined as suited for life. All 12 stars are single, nonfluctuating, slowly rotating dwarfs residing on the main sequence for lifetimes of from about seven to 30 or 40 billion years, ample time for the evolution of life to take place.[109]

How accurate is fish's analysis?

Fish's efforts and dedication are commendable, but we must remain objective in our analysis and must question the validity of her method and conclusion. Fish's star model was criticized by Carl Sagan and Steve Soter in the December 1974 issue of the journal *Astronomy*. Sagan and Soter argued that if one omits the lines between the stars from Betty's sketch, the map shows very little resemblance to Zeta Reticulum. Furthermore, the authors contend that the stars Fish chose to include in her data were deliberately chosen to resemble Betty's star map, and thus Fish went into the project with a predetermined idea. Adding to this, if one looks at Betty's sketch, there are several "random dots scattered about," but only three of these dots appear in the map Fish used for comparison, while others were omitted. This further consolidates Sagan and Soter's argument, that some stars were intentionally selected whereas others were dismissed.

Moreover, we can note further inconsistencies and errors in Fish's model if we look at the data provided by Hipparcos, the European Space Agency satellite which explored accurate measurements of celestial bodies in the sky. By using data from Hipparcos, we are now aware of the fact that some of the stars on the map are further away than Fish had presumed. Furthermore, we also know that some of the stars in Fish's selection cannot possibly support the evolution of life, whereas some of the stars she dismissed can.

> The argument on "The Zeta Reticuli Incident" demonstrates only that if we set out to find a pattern correlation between two nearly random data sets by selecting at will certain elements from each and ignoring others, we will always be successful.[110]

---

[109] Walter Webb, "An Analysis of the Fish Model", (Durham, NH: University of New Hampshire Library, 1961), 4.

[110] Carl Sagan and Steven Soter, "Pattern Recognition and Zeta Reticuli," *Astronomy*, December 1974.

Betty's star map is undeniably intriguing and over the years has added further mystery to this abduction case. However, if we use the data we have at our disposal presently, we must acknowledge that Fish's model and conclusions are inaccurate. With that being said, many skeptics have used this fact to argue that the entire case is a hoax, but such a conclusion is an unfounded one. We must keep in mind that both in her dream journal and in the hypnotic regression sessions, Betty never claimed that the star map was of Zeta Reticulum; she had simply made a sketch of the map she saw on board to the best of her recollection. It was only after Fish's analysis that it became a "well known fact" that the extraterrestrials originated from Zeta Reticulum. The next piece of evidence we shall analyze is Betty's blue dress, the same dress she wore that night of the encounter.

The blue dress

> Later, when I was cleaning out my closet, I found my dress. When I removed it from the closet, I noticed it was covered with a pink, powdery substance. I was puzzled by this and checked the rest of my clothing to see if any others might have this substance on them. No, only my dress.[111]

If we go back to the timeline of events, when Betty was placed on the metallic table and the examiner was trying to take off her dress, he caused a tear at the zipper region. Years later, this tear proved to be a significant piece of evidence in the case. As they arrived back at home in Portsmouth after the encounter, Betty took off the blue dress, folded it and placed it at the back of her closet. Later on, as she was cleaning out her closet and clothes, she noticed that the blue dress was the only piece of clothing in the closet which was covered in a pink powdery substance. She tried removing the pink powder, but it had stained, so she put it in the bin. It wasn't until the memories began to resurface and she remembered that the examiner had torn it that she realized that

---

[111] Betty Hill, "My Blue Dress" (Durham, NH: University of New Hampshire Library, 1961), 4.

this dress was a critical piece of evidence and could provide additional corroboration.

Betty ran back and retrieved the dress and inspected it closely. Upon inspecting it further, she noticed that the dress had multiple tears: the built-in lining was badly torn, as was the seam down the center of the back of the lining. Moreover, the dress's hem was torn and there were two tears at the zipper, a one-inch tear on the left side and a two-inch tear on the right side. After these discoveries, Betty placed the dress on a hanger and covered it in plastic and placed it back in her closet.

In 1978, Betty met Dr. Leonard Stringfield, and as she told him of these discoveries, he insisted the dress be sent in for analysis. The blue dress was then handed over to Dubois Chemicals in Cincinnati, Ohio, and was analyzed by Professor Harry Mark Jr. and Wayne Robbins. The pair made some significant discoveries that will be investigated further, one of which being that despite using several methods that would normally cause discoloration or staining, they were unable to replicate the pink powder stain found on the dress. Their report states:

1. Direct analysis by X-ray fluorescence showed no difference in elemental composition of the front and back samples.
2. One-inch squares, from each of the front and back were digested with a concentrated nitric acid-sulfuric acid mixture. The resulting solutions were analyzed by emission spectroscopy (a much more sensitive test than 1). Traces of copper, calcium, silicon, magnesium and iron were found, but were essentially the same in both front and back samples.
3. Several methods which normally bleach or discolor cloth dyes were tried in an attempt to duplicate the color change observed on the dress. These were (a) chlorine bleach (both wet and dry), (b) acid treatment, (c) base treatment, (d) ultraviolet light (one day exposure) and (e) sunlamp (one day exposure). The closest was acid treatment which bleached it white, but not red. This is interesting even though it is not a negative result. It shows that whatever the reaction was, it was not the usual discoloration reactions that I know.[112]

The dress was analyzed once more, this time in 2001 by P. A. Budinger, an analytical scientist at Frontier Analysis Limited. Budinger first

---

[112] Harry Mark (Cincinnati, OH, 1978).

examined the dress's structure and noted that it was made of a common sheath-like style with a printed design in various shades of blue. The dress had short sleeves, a natural waist, and a straight skirt. Budinger noted the extensive discoloration along the top half of the dress, particularly the underarms and the bottom half. Budinger then went on to analyze two samples from the dress: a discolored sample (DS) which was taken from the discolored area of the dress, and a control sample (CS) which was taken from a different part of the dress that had retained its original color. Budinger concluded:

a) The DS suffered chemical effects on both the dye and the fiber.
b) The DS contained more particulate material than the CS.
c) The fabric of the DS was coated with a biologically derived material which was composed mostly of protein and a small amount of glycerol ester.
d) The biologically derived material originated from an external source (as opposed to a natural source, such as vomit, urine or perspiration).
e) The DS had a more acidic pH level than the CS.

These analyses are yet another piece of critical evidence in the Betty and Barney case and demonstrate that:

a) The researchers were unable to identify what the pink powder was.
b) The researchers were unable to replicate the stain on the dress.
c) The researchers ruled out the possibility that the stain was made by Betty herself.

Hypotheses

As one can see, the Betty and Barney case has a wealth of evidence, which is what makes this case so compelling and fascinating. In this part of the chapter, we will explore the possible hypotheses.

Hypothesis #1: Just a UFO sighting

The first hypothesis we shall explore follows the conclusion made by psychiatrist Dr. Simon. Before we explore this hypothesis, it is important to first explore his stance on the UFO phenomenon. In a letter written in 1975 addressed to Philip J. Klass, a renowned UFO skeptic, Dr. Simon mentioned that he had two UFO sightings of his own, and although he believed that it was possible to have visitors from outer space, the likelihood of this happening was highly unlikely.

After Dr. Simon finished the hypnosis sessions with the Hills, he was of the opinion that Betty and Barney did indeed witness a UFO, but the abduction and examinations had not truly taken place. The UFO sighting had made Betty feel anxious, and this anxiety manifested itself in her nightmares. Furthermore, as Betty told Barney about her dreams, he subconsciously retained these details and recalled similar ones himself while under hypnosis. Dr. Simon went on to say that Barney's experience could also be a manifestation of his "racial paranoia." These points are certainly valid and noteworthy. The Hills did indeed witness a UFO which was corroborated by several other independent reports and radar sightings. It was also the case that Betty was anxious as a result of the sighting, and Barney, understandably, did experience paranoia. However, does this sufficiently explain their encounter? Could it be that the details mentioned in the hypnotic regression sessions were simply a manifestation of anxiety and did not actually occur? Lastly, is it possible that Barney's narrative was influenced by Betty's nightmares, coupled with his cultural paranoia?

Looking back at the story, Betty did mention her nightmares to Barney, but he dismissed them as "just dreams," and following that comment, Betty did not bring them up again. While I do think that Betty's dreams could have influenced Barney's hypnosis, I do not think that the narrative can be reduced to "racial paranoia" and anxiety. Furthermore, this hypothesis does not take into account several factors, such as the missing time period, the magnetic field surrounding the car, the growths around Barney's groin region, and the findings on the blue dress Betty was wearing.

Hypothesis #2: The extraterrestrial hypothesis

There are several factors which support the extraterrestrial hypothesis: the theory that Betty and Barney were abducted by an extraterrestrial entity and were subjected to medical experiments on board the aircraft. The first factor is the fact that the UFO they saw was in all likelihood an extraterrestrial aircraft since it possessed several of the five observables aforementioned in this book. The aircraft had a disk shape and lacked flight characteristics such as wings. It also did not have a visible propulsion system and it performed instantaneous accelerations and incredible maneuvers. The second factor which supports this hypothesis is the missing time period, which is, as we have seen in many of the cases explored in this book, a common phenomenon among abductees. Moreover, it is possible that the magnetic field surrounding the car and the silver spots on its surface were caused by the disk's propulsion system.

Another factor which supports this hypothesis is the immediate and intermediate aftereffects reported by Betty and Barney. It is difficult to attribute the physiological ailments they suffered (most notably the growths in Barney's groin region) to a mere coincidence. The last factor which corroborates the extraterrestrial hypothesis is Betty's blue dress and the analyses which were performed on it. Given the substantial amount of evidence presented, can we conclude that this was indeed a close encounter of the fourth kind?

Conclusion

After reviewing the case details, it is evident why the Betty and Barney Hill case is one of the most credible and best documented cases of an alien abduction. There are many corroborative factors which cannot be ignored or dismissed. While the Hills did indeed gain fame and publicity from the encounter, it was not their initial intention. In fact, their encounter was leaked to the media without their permission by someone close to the case, and it was from there that the case gained notoriety and became the most well-known abduction case. After presenting all of the facts and evidence in this chapter, it is now up to you, the reader, to form your own informed opinion. Is it possible that the Hills were abducted by an extraterrestrial entity, or are there rational explanations for what happened that night?

CHAPTER 14

Conclusion

As we saw earlier in the book, science has now provided us with enough data and information for us to conclude that it is highly unlikely that human beings are the only intelligent life-form in the universe. The probability that we share the cosmos with other intelligent and conscious beings is astronomical. Thus, is the idea of an alien abduction so far-fetched? I personally believe that these entities appear to view us in the same way we view other species. Despite the fact that it is unethical, humans have been capturing and keeping animals in laboratories for decades, experimenting on them, and exploiting them in order to better understand behavior and anatomy. As we have seen in the cases presented in this section, similarly, these beings capture, observe, and experiment on humans in order to better understand our nature, behavior, and psyche.

AFTERWORD

The more time passes, the more willing people have become to discuss the UFO phenomenon and what is considered "paranormal." Just because a phenomenon or event cannot be explained by conventional science does not mean that it does not occur or that it is a hoax. In the past, we have made numerous discoveries that were once thought to be improbable from a scientific standpoint, for example, the discovery of black holes. Having said that, we must now acknowledge that we have entered a new era in the study of UFOs. Looking back at previous investigations into UFO sightings carried out by the Air Force, such as Project Sign and Project Blue Book, the cases were mostly given the same explanation, and the extraterrestrial hypothesis was rarely even considered. We are now at a point in history where the government has publicly acknowledged the existence of UAPs as well as the fact that these unidentified aircraft are equipped with advanced technology that we cannot yet fully comprehend.

In my first book, *Evidence of Extraterrestrials: Over 40 Cases Prove Aliens Have Visited Earth*, I explored the most significant UFO sightings, and the writing and the publication of the book coincided with the government's acknowledgment of the existence of the phenomenon.

After finishing writing my first book, there were many more aspects of the phenomenon that I wanted to research and write about, and that was how the material for this book came about. Close encounters have always piqued my interest, but as has been mentioned throughout this book, there's much more to alien abductions than just a captivating narrative. There are a number of implications which affect us collectively as human beings, which I will now briefly explore.

Implication #1: Ontological shock

From a young age, many of us are taught that life exists solely on Earth and that human beings are the superior species on this planet. Sadly, this superiority complex is mirrored in many of our behaviors: we capture animals and keep them in laboratories for testing, we slaughter millions of animals for our consumption and are continuously depleting the planet's natural resources. We are a destructive species, and this sense of self-importance can be traced back to Genesis 1:26, which says:

> Then God said, "Let us make mankind in our image, in our likeness, so that they may rule over the fish in the sea and the birds in the sky, over the livestock and all the wild animals, and over all the creatures that move along the ground."

We may believe that humans rule over every creature on Earth, but if extraterrestrials exist, have been visiting Earth, and have been capturing human beings for their own benefit, how valid is this belief? These beings have proven that they are infinitely more advanced than us, which means that we are not the superior species after all, making us question everything we were previously taught. Quite frankly, many of the cases covered in this book show how little control we do actually have: abductees are always taken without their consent, are subjected to intrusive medical experiments, and then, once these beings have observed enough and gained what they needed, they return the individual in an induced amnesiac state. So, I must ask: if such an advanced, conscious, and powerful life-form exists elsewhere in the universe, what makes human beings so special? What do we have left to show that we are the superior species?

Implication #2: The human anatomy and psyche

The second implication is that for some reason beyond our knowledge, extraterrestrials are deeply interested in our anatomy and psyche. This can be seen in the majority of alien abduction cases we have covered in this book as the abductee is subjected to a number of examinations. These beings have also shown interest in our psyche and emotions, especially in the way we process fear and anxiety. As these cases have demonstrated, close encounters are as much about the psyche and our collective consciousness as they are about the physical body. What the reason behind this interest is, however, we do not know.

Implication #3: Preservation

The third and final implication we shall discuss is the idea of preservation. First, in many of the abduction cases, contactees have reportedly received a warning—a warning of what will happen to Earth if our self-destructive behavior remains unchanged. Contactees are frequently shown telepathic images and are told that we must protect our planet, as we are slowly eradicating it. Second, for one reason or another, these beings seem to have a purpose for us and would prefer that we do not go extinct or destroy planet Earth, which makes sense given that Earth is part of a larger system that could, in turn, affect them as well. This idea is supported by many of the cases discussed in my first book, in which I explore several sightings that took place over nuclear missile sites; on numerous occasions, UFOs have directly interfered with the operation of nuclear weapons, and many UFO sightings have occurred over restricted military airspace, implying that these entities are monitoring our military activity.

These are just three of the many implications, and they highlight why this phenomenon is so important and why we must continue to study it in order to better understand it. Like I said, this isn't just about a fascinating narrative of an individual getting abducted. That is, of course, intriguing, but when we look closer and analyze it, we can see that it is much larger than that. There's so much more to it.

The cases I mentioned in this book are what I believe to be the most significant and compelling accounts of close encounters of the third and fourth kind. There could be several others that I may be unaware of, which could be just as, if not even more, credible. This journey of exploration is an ongoing one, and I encourage you, the reader, to continue on this journey. As you explore this phenomenon further, you are also exploring the cosmos and the secrets it holds.

I hope you have approached this book and phenomenon with an open mind—the goal of this book is not to persuade skeptics that aliens exist and abductions take place. The facts speak for themselves. Rather, it is to continue the dialogue about the existence of extraterrestrials and the implications of this phenomenon. The question is no longer whether they exist or if they are here or not, but rather: *why do they need us?* Throughout the writing of this book I found myself asking this question multiple times. If these beings are so advanced, then why are we so important to them? If there is life elsewhere in the universe, what is so special about Earth?

We may never have the answers to these questions, but as Stanton Friedman told me, they are here for their own purposes, not ours. We may never truly comprehend certain aspects of the phenomenon, nor do I expect to—this phenomenon is so complex and vast that it is simply impossible to do so. I have come to accept that uncertainties and mysteries are unavoidable when dealing with such an existential prospect. What we do conclusively know, however, is that the cosmos is teeming with life and with possibilities, and in a universe that is infinite, there are infinite possibilities. What is also certain is that we are not alone, we never have been, and for some reason or another, our cosmic brothers have a keen interest in us and in our planet. I stress, they are here for their own purposes, not ours.

BIBLIOGRAPHY

APRO (1976, October 6). The Kentucky Abduction. *The APRO Bulletin,* 24(6).

Ariel School UFO Landing (1994). YouTube, https://youtube.com/watch?v=eBqKJHSrYZg (last accessed January 9, 2023).

Barrett, J. (1987). Polygraph Examination of Whitley Strieber—18th May 1987. *Unknown Country,* May 1987. https://unknowncountry.com/wp-content/uploads/2019/03/lonpoly.jpg (last accessed November 12, 2023).

Blum, R., & Blum, J. (1974). *Beyond Earth: Man's Contact with UFOs.* New York: Bantam.

Bob Lazar: Area 51 & Flying Saucers (2018). Documentary. Directed by J. K. L. Corbell.

Breakthrough Initiatives (2015, July 20). Launch of Breakthrough Initiatives. https://breakthroughinitiatives.org/events/4 (last accessed January 10, 2023).

Brummett, W., & Zuick, E. (1974). Should the USAF Reopen Project Blue Book? Dissertation, Air University, Maxwell Air Force Base.

Budinger, P., & Budinger, B. (2017). *Analysis of Soil Samples from the Travis Walton Abduction Site (Apache Sitgreaves National Forest, Near Heber Arizona).* Report. Frontier Analysis Ltd.

Campbell, S. (1979). Close Encounter in Scotland. *Journal of Transient Aerial Phenomena, 1*(2).

Campbell, S. (1986). Livingston: A New Hypothesis. *Journal of Transient Aerial Phenomena, 4*(3).

Clark, J. (1996). *High Strangeness: UFOs from 1960 Through 1979*. Detroit, MI: Omnigraphics.

Clark, J. (1998). *The UFO Book: Encyclopedia of the Extraterrestrial*. Detroit, MI: Visible Ink Press.

Conselice, C., Wilkinson, A., Duncan, K., & Mortlock, A. (2016). The Evolution of Galaxy Number Density at z < 8 and its Implications. *Astrophysical Journal*, October.

Condon, E. (1969). *Final Report of the Scientific Study of Unidentified Flying Objects*. New York: Bantam.

Cooper, H., Blumenthal, R., & Kean, L. (2017, December 16). Glowing Auras and "Black Money": The Pentagon's Mysterious U.F.O. Program. *The New York Times*. https://nytimes.com/2017/12/16/us/politics/pentagon-program-ufo-harry-reid.html (last accessed January 10, 2023).

da Silva, T. Jn., & Foy, R. (1987). Zeta 1 and Zeta 2 Reticuli: A Puzzling Solar-Type Twin System. *Astronomy and Astrophysics, 177*: 204–216.

Defense Intelligence Agency (2009). Defense Intelligence Reference Document. Review of Anomalous Acute and Subacute Field Effects on Human Biological Tissues. https://dia.mil/FOIA/FOIA-Electronic-Reading-Room/FileId/170026/ (last accessed January 10, 2023).

Defense Intelligence Agency (2019). Antigraivty for Aerospace Application. Advanced Aerospace Weapon System Applications.

Drake, F. D., & Sobel, D. (1992). *Is Anyone Out There? The Scientific Search for Extraterrestrial Intelligence*. New York: Delacorte.

Duane, M. (1986). Psychological Report. *Unknown Country*, March 1986. https://unknowncountry.com/wp-content/uploads/2019/03/nytest1.jpg (last accessed January 9, 2024).

European Space Agency (2004, March 8). Hubble Sees Galaxies Galore. https://sci.esa.int/web/hubble/-/34828-hubble-sees-galaxies-galore (last accessed January 10, 2023).

Federal Bureau of Investigation (1964). Review of *Unidentified Flying Object; Socorro, New Mexico; April 24, 1964. The Black Vault*. https://documents2.theblackvault.com/documents/fbifiles/paranormal/FBI-UFO-Socorro-fbi1.pdf (last accessed March 22, 2023).

GEIPAN (1965). Commandement Regional De la Gendarmerie De La 9° Region Militaire. Review of Procès-Verbal N° 105 Du 2 Juillet 1965. https://geipan.fr/sites/default/files/PV%20n%C2%B0445%20%281965309761%29.pdf (last accessed April 16, 2023).

Henderson, P. (1961, September 20). *Air Intelligence Information Report; 100-1-61—Unidentified Flying Object.*

Hickson, C., & Mendez, W. (1983). *UFO Contact at Pascagoula*. Gig Harbor, WA: Wendelle C. Stevens.

Hill, B. (n.d.). Dreams or Recall? Folder 2, Box 4, Betty and Barney Hill Papers, 1961–2006. MC 197. Milne Special Collections and Archives, University of New Hampshire Library, Durham, NH.

Hill, B. (n.d.). Hypnosis Transcripts, Sessions 1–9. Folder 8, Box 5, Betty and Barney Hill Papers, 1961–2006. MC 197. Milne Special Collections and Archives, University of New Hampshire Library, Durham, NH.

Hind, C. (1995a). UFO Flap in Zimbabwe. *UFO AFRINEWS, 11* (February).

Hind, C. (1995b). Recent UFO Sightings in Africa—The Cultural Implications. *UFOs: Examining the Evidence: The Proceedings of 8th BUFORA International UFO Congress*. https://bufora.org.uk/documents/1995 UFOsExaminingtheevidence.8thInternationalconference.pdf (last accessed January 9, 2023).

Hough, P. A., & Moyshe, K. (1997). *The Truth about Alien Abductions*. New York: Sterling.

Hunt, S. E. (Department of Health and Welfare) (1967). Determination of Possible Radiation Hazards to the General Public from the Alleged Landing Site of an Unidentified Flying Object near Falcon Lake, Manitoba. Library and Archives Canada, September. https://bac-lac. gc.ca/eng/discover/unusual/ufo/Documents/1967-09-13.pdf (last accessed May 3, 2023).

Hynek, J. A. (1998). *The UFO Experience: A Scientific Inquiry*. New York: Marlowe.

Institute of Medicine, Board on the Health of Select Populations, and Committee on the Assessment of Ongoing Efforts in the Treatment of Post-traumatic Stress Disorder. (2014). *Treatment for Post-Traumatic Stress Disorder in Military and Veteran Populations: Initial Assessment*. Washington, DC: National Academies Press.

Klass, P. J. (1975–76). Letters to Dr. Benjamin Simon. October 28, 1975 and March 1, 1976.

Klass, P. J. (1983). *UFOs: The Public Deceived*. New York: Prometheus.

Kricheff, I., & Seidenwurm, D. (1988). Magnetic Resonance Imaging of the Brain. *Unknown Country*, March 1988. https://unknowncountry.com/ wp-content/uploads/2019/03/mri.jpg (last accessed November 12, 2023).

Laurendi, N. (1988). Polygraph Examination of Whitley Strieber. *Unknown Country*, March 1988. https://unknowncountry.com/wp-content/ uploads/2019/03/nypoly1.jpg (last accessed November 12, 2023).

Lazar, B. (2019). *Dreamland: An Autobiography*. Cardiff by the Sea, CA: Interstellar.

Man Says Brother Spent 5 Days on UFO (1971, November 12). *The Arizona Daily Star*.

Marrs, J. (1997). *Alien Agenda: Investigating the Extraterrestrial Presence Among Us.* New York: HarperCollins.

Marden, K. (2007). *Captured!—The Betty and Barney Hill UFO Experience: The True Story of the World's First Documented Alien Abduction.* Newburyport, MA: Red Wheel/Weiser.

Mack, J. E. (2011). *Passport to the Cosmos: Human Transformation and Alien Encounters.* Guildford, UK: White Crow.

Mark, H. (1978, May 11). Letter to Dr. Leonard Stringfield. Cincinnati, OH: University of Cincinnati.

Mellon, C. (2018). The military keeps encountering UFOs. Why doesn't the Pentagon care? *The Washington Post.* March. https://washingtonpost.com/outlook/the-military-keeps-encountering-ufos-why-doesnt-the-pentagon-care/2018/03/09/242c125c-22ee-11e8-94da-ebf9d112159c_story.html (last accessed January 10, 2023).

Michel, A. (1965). The Valensole Affair. *Flying Saucer Review*, 11(6).

Michel, A., & Bowen, C. (1968). A Visit to Valensole. *Flying Saucer Review*, 14(1).

Michalak, S., Rutkowski, C. A., & Michalak, S. (2018). *When They Appeared: Falcon Lake 1967: The Inside Story of a Close Encounter.* Guildford, UK: August Night.

NASA (2012, December 9). Hubble Goes to the eXtreme to Assemble Farthest-Ever View of the Universe. https://nasa.gov/mission_pages/hubble/science/xdf.html (last accessed July 10, 2023).

NASA Goddard Media Studios (2015). Review of NASM 2015: Our Violent Universe. https://svs.gsfc.nasa.gov/12027 (last accessed July 10, 2023).

National Enquirer, The (1975, December 16). Arizona Man Captured by UFO.

Norman, E. (1973). *Gods and Devils from Outer Space.* New York: Lancer.

Office of the Director of National Intelligence (2021). Preliminary Assessment: Unidentified Aerial Phenomena. https://dni.gov/files/ODNI/documents/assessments/Prelimary-Assessment-UAP-20210625.pdf (last accessed January 10, 2023).

Oganessian, Y. T., & Utyonkov, V. K. 2015. Super-heavy element research. *Reports on Progress in Physics*, 78(3): 036301.

Parker, C. (2018). *Pascagoula: The Closest Encounter: My Story.* Pontefract, UK: Flying Disk Press.

Pedley, T. (1986). EEG Report. *Unknown Country*, December 1986. https://unknowncountry.com/wp-content/uploads/2019/03/eeg.jpg (last accessed November 12, 2023).

Permanent Select Committee on Intelligence: Subcommittee on Counterterrorism, Counterintelligence, and Counterproliferation. (2022). *Unidentified Aerial Phenomena D545.* Vol. D545. Congressional Record—Daily Digest, May 17, 2022. https://govinfo.gov/content/pkg/

CREC-2022-05-17/pdf/CREC-2022-05-17-pt1-PgD545-2.pdf#page=1 (last accessed January 10, 2023).

Peters, W. (2013). Louise Smith/Kentucky Women Abduction. In: *Factual Eyewitness Testimony of UFO Encounters*. Music album.

Porto de Mello, G., Fernandez del Peloso, E., & Ghezzi, L. (2006). Astrobiologically Interesting Stars within 10 Parsecs of the Sun. *Astrobiology*, 6(2): 308–331. https://doi.org/10.1089/ast.2006.6.308 (last accessed November 23, 2022).

Project Blue Book, 1947–1969. (2022). Fold3 database with images. https://fold3.com/publication/461/project-blue-book-ufo-investigations (last accessed November 21, 2022).

Quintanilla, H. (1981). Fall 1966: 4-37-3: The Investigation of UFOs, by Hector Quintanilla, Jr. http://catalog.archives.gov/id/7282832 (last accessed October 12 , 2022).

Randles, J. (1997). *The Truth Behind Men in Black: Government Agents, or Visitors from Beyond*. New York: St. Martin's.

Robinson, M. (2019). *The Dechmont Woods UFO Incident (An Ordinary Day, An Extraordinary Event)*. lulu.com.

Rotaru, T.-Ş., & Rusu, A. (2015). A Meta-Analysis for the Efficacy of Hypnotherapy in Alleviating PTSD Symptoms. *International Journal of Clinical and Experimental Hypnosis*, 64(1): 116–136. https://doi.org/10.1080/00207144.2015.1099406 (last accessed November 23, 2022).

Royal Canadian Mounted Police. (1967). Stefan Michalak—Report of Unidentified Flying Object, Falcon Beach, Manitoba. 20 May 67. Library and Archives Canada. https://bac-lac.gc.ca/eng/discover/unusual/ufo/Documents/1967-06-18.pdf (last accessed July 17, 2023).

Sagan, C., & Soter, S. (1974). Pattern Recognition and Zeta Reticuli. *Astronomy*, December.

Stewart, K. (1999). Psychological Evaluation. *Unknown Country*, January 1999. https://unknowncountry.com/wp-content/uploads/2019/03/txtest1.jpg (last accessed November 12, 2023).

Strieber, W. (1988). *Communion: A True Story*. New York: Avon.

Stringfield, L. (1977). The Stanford, Kentucky Abduction. *The MUFON UFO Journal*, 110: 5–15.

Sullivan, W. (1970). *We Are Not Alone: The Search for Intelligent Life on Other Worlds*. New York: McGraw-Hill.

Synnott, J., Dietzel, D., & Ioannou, M. (2015). A review of the polygraph: history, methodology and current status. Crime Psychology Review, 1: 1, 59–83. DOI: 10.1080/23744006.2015.1060080 (last accessed November 23, 2022).

The One Show. (2020, February 26). BBC Television programme.

The Schoolkids Who Said They Saw "Aliens". (2021, July 10). BBC. https://bbc.com/news/av/stories-57749238 (last accessed January 9, 2023).

Thomas, D. (2001). A Different Angle on the Socorro UFO of 1964. *Skeptical Inquirer*, 25(4): 5–12.

"UFOs." (1980, November 4). Episode. *Arthur C. Clarke's Mysterious World*. ITV Network.

Vallée, J. (1990). *Confrontations: A Scientist's Search for Alien Contact*. New York: Ballantine.

Walton, T. (1996). *Fire in the Sky: The Walton Experience*. Boston, MA: Da Capo.

Webb, W. (1965). A Dramatic UFO Encounter in the White Mountains, New Hampshire, The Hill Case—September 19–20, 1961. NICAP, September 1965. http://nicap.org/reports/610919hill_report2.pdf (last accessed November 23, 2022).

Webb, W. (n.d.). "Analysis of the Fish Model", Folder 1, Box 6, Betty and Barney Hill Papers, 1961–2006. MC 197, Milne Special Collections and Archives, University of New Hampshire Library, Durham, NH.

Wiser, C. (n.d., a). Ariel School—First on the Scene. *Three-Dollar Kit*. https://threedollarkit.weebly.com/ariel-first-on-the-scene.html (last accessed January 09, 2024).

Wiser, C. (n.d., b). Dr John Mack Interviews. Three-Dollar Kit. https://threedollarkit.weebly.com/ariel-mack.html (last accessed January 9, 2023).

Wiser, C. (2022). Ariel TV Interviews. *Three-Dollar Kit*. https://threedollarkit.weebly.com/ariel-tv-interviews.html (last accessed January 9, 2023).

ABOUT THE AUTHOR

Warren Agius is a longtime UFO researcher, known for his unbiased approach to factual evidence. He is the author of *Evidence of Extraterrestrials: Over 40 Cases Prove Aliens Have Visited Earth.*

INDEX

www.ingramcontent.com/pod-product-compliance
Lightning Source LLC
Jackson TN
JSHW030738101224
76011JS00012B/65

* 9 7 8 1 8 0 1 5 2 1 4 1 3 *